MW00967428

NASCAR

DAILY
DEVOTIONS
FOR
DIE-HARD
FANS

NASCAR

NASCAR

Daily Devotions for Die-Hard Fans: NASCAR
Second Edition © 2010 Ed McMinn

All rights reserved, including the right to reproduce this book or portions thereof in any form whatsoever.

Library of Congress Cataloging-in-Publication Data
13 ISBN Digit ISBN: 978-0-9801749-3-9

Manufactured in the United States of America.

Unless otherwise noted, scripture quotations are taken from the *Holy Bible, New International Version.* Copyright © 1973, 1978, 1984, by the International Bible Society. All rights reserved.

For bulk purchases or to request the author for speaking engagements, email contact@extrapointpublishers.com.

Go to http://www.die-hardfans.com for information about other titles in the series.

Cover and interior design by Slynn McMinn.

Every effort has been made to identify copyright holders. Any omissions are wholly unintentional. Extra Point Publishers should be notified in writing immediately for full acknowledgement in future editions.

NASCAR

*To Ralph Johnson,
who lives with God at the wheel*

DAY 1

IN THE BEGINNING

Read Genesis 1, 2:1-3.

"God saw all that he had made, and it was very good" (v. 1:31).

Bootleggers racing in a field on Sundays to determine who had the fastest car. According to Tim Flock, "That was the very start of stock car racing."

Flock won thirty-nine races between 1949 and 1961, including eighteen in 1955. He was present at the creation, witnessing stock car racing's colorful beginnings that arose from the desperation of the Depression and men having families to feed.

His brothers Bob and Fonty were moonshine runners. "You could buy liquor legal, but this was during the Depression and people didn't have enough money to buy government liquor," Flock explained. Men couldn't find jobs that paid decent wages so making the whiskey and transporting the whiskey were ways to put food on the table.

Flock never hauled any liquor himself as his older brothers kept him in school, but he was around the bootlegging. "There were between twenty and thirty bootleggers running two or three loads a day out of Dahlonega, Georgia, up in the north Georgia mountains, to Atlanta," Flock remembered.

He recalled that his brothers and other bootleggers got to arguing one day about who had the fastest car, and they decided to settle the dispute in a field outside Atlanta. "They started racing those bootleg cars on Sunday and betting against each other," Flock said. And then something surprising happened: People showed up to watch the races. "The bootleggers would pass the old helmets around the fence and the spectators'd put quarters in them, half dollars, and the drivers'd collect quite a bit of money on Sunday afternoons," Flock said.

A man named Bill France heard about the crowds and built some half-mile tracks. The rest is sports history.

Beginnings are important, but what we make of them is even more important. Consider, for example, how far NASCAR has come since those bootleggers got together for some Sunday afternoon bragging.

Every morning, you get a gift from God: a new beginning. God hands to you as an expression of divine love a new day full of promise and the chance to right the wrongs in your life. You can use the day to pay a debt, start a new relationship, replace a burned-out light bulb, tell your family you love them, chase a dream, solve a nagging problem . . . or not.

God simply provides the gift. How you use it is up to you. People often talk wistfully about starting over or making a new beginning. God gives you the chance with the dawning of every new day. You have the chance today to make things right – and that includes your relationship with God.

Racing cars began the day they built the second automobile.
-- Richard Petty

Every day is not just a dawn; it is a precious chance to start over or begin anew.

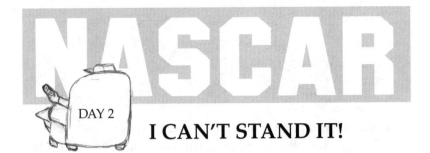

I CAN'T STAND IT!

Read Exodus 32:1-20.

"[Moses'] anger burned and he threw the tablets out of his hands, breaking them to pieces at the foot of the mountain" (v. 19).

One writer called it "one of the most frustrating streaks ever in NASCAR history." It belonged to Dale Earnhardt.

Nineteen years in a row, one of the sport's greatest drivers fell short in the biggest race of all; he couldn't win the Daytona 500. "The harder he tried, the more frustrated he became," wrote Jerry Bonkowski about Earnhardt's streak. Joe Menzer called the streak "a one-thousand-pound gorilla." Earnhardt won everywhere else; he'd even won at Daytona 33 times, including an unbelievable streak of ten 125-mile qualifying races in a row. But the seven-time Cup champion had never won the 500.

It wasn't like Earnhardt didn't have his chances; it was just that something always seemed to happen. Perhaps the strangest "something" of all was a sea gull. One year Earnhardt was running up front when he slammed into a sea gull and was knocked out of the race. In 1986, he was leading late in the race when he ran out of gas. In 1990, he was leading on the last lap when he ran into some debris, which jammed his radiator and cut a tire. He finished fifth. In 1993, he again was leading late when Dale Jarrett passed him for the win.

It got so bad that when Earnhardt came to Daytona in 1998,

he "had all but given up on his dream. He was resigned to let whatever happened happen." What happened was that the streak ended. On his twentieth try, at age 47, The Intimidator claimed the checkered flag. "Every crew member of every team ventured onto pit road to shake his hand as he drove to victory lane." In celebration, Earnhardt did doughnuts in the infield, trying to dig out his number three in the dirt.

The frustration was over and done with.

The traffic light catches you when you're running late for work or your doctor's appointment. The bureaucrat gives you red tape when you want assistance. Your daughter refuses to take her homework seriously. Makes your blood boil, doesn't it?

Frustration is part of God's testing ground that is life even if much of what frustrates us today results from man-made organizations, bureaucracies, and machines. What's important is not that you encounter frustration—that's a given—but how you handle it. Do you respond with curses, screams, and violence? Or with a deep breath, a silent prayer, and calm persistence, and patience?

It may be difficult to imagine Jesus stuck in traffic or waiting for hours in a long line in a government office. It is not difficult, however, to imagine how he would act in such situations, and, thus, to know exactly how you should respond. No matter how frustrated you are.

I've got that monkey off my back!
-- Dale Earnhardt after his 1998 win at Daytona

**Frustration is a vexing part of life,
but God expects us to handle it gracefully.**

SPREADING THE WORD

Read Mark 1:21-28.

"News about him spread quickly over the whole region"
(v. 28).

Carl Edwards got his start as a driver because he followed the old adage "It pays to advertise."

Edwards exploded onto the NASCAR scene in 2005 when he won at Atlanta Motor Speedway in just the fourth race of his first full season. He passed Jimmie Johnson off the final turn of the final lap to earn that first win. He celebrated that victory -- and subsequent ones - with what became his signature: a back flip off his car.

Edwards discovered his love for racing when he was 17 and went to work in a cousin's shop. "That kind of turned racing into a reality for me," Edwards said as he helped out at the shop and then helped the shop guys when they raced on the weekend.

He drove dirt-track modifieds, all the while looking for a way to get his foot into NASCAR's door. His mom came up with an idea, telling him, "You need a business card that says you want to drive race cars." Edwards liked the idea, went to a print shop, and had some cards printed up. "It was like $100 for 2,000 business cards with my picture on them," Edwards remembered.

And so everywhere he went he handed out cards. "I figured eventually the whole world would know that I wanted to drive race cars and there would be some owner that would need a driver," Edwards said. Sure enough, in 2003 Roush Racing needed a Truck Series driver, and Edwards got his shot. He won three races and was the rookie of the year.

Carl Edwards didn't need to advertise anymore.

Commercials and advertisements for products and services inundate us. Turn on your computer: ads pop up. Watch NASCAR: decals cover the cars and the drivers' uniforms. TV, radio, newspapers, billboards -- everyone's trying to spread the word in the best way possible.

Jesus was no different in that he used the most effective and efficient means of advertising he had at his disposal to spread his message of salvation and hope among the masses. That was word of mouth.

In his ministry, Jesus didn't isolate himself; instead, he moved from town to town among the common people, preaching, teaching, and healing. Those who encountered Jesus then told others about their experience, thus spreading the word about the good news.

Almost two millennia later, nothing's really changed. Speaking to someone else about Jesus remains the best way to get the word out, and the best advertisement of all is a changed life.

Everywhere I went I always had business cards. I figured somebody would say, "Man, you ought to hire him."
-- Carl Edwards

The best advertising for Jesus is word of mouth, telling others what He has done for you.

DAY 4

SUPERSTITION

Read 1 Samuel 28:3-20.

*"Saul then said to his attendants, 'Find me a woman who
is a medium, so I may go and inquire of her'" (v. 7).*

None of these present-day guys seem superstitious," hall-of-
fame crew chief Waddell Wilson once remarked about NASCAR's
21st-century drivers. The same cannot be said of drivers of an
earlier generation.

For instance, when racing pioneer Louise Smith drove at
Daytona in 1947, the drivers had to draw for their position because
of rain. Smith drew thirteen: "Unlucky thirteen. I tried to swap
that thirteen . . . all down and up the line. No one would trade me.
Nobody wanted that thing. They were scared about that thirteen."
So Smith kept it -- and wrecked, tearing up the only car she had.

Joe Weatherly refused to run in the Southern 500 at Darlington
in 1962 because it was the thirteenth staging of what was then
NASCAR's biggest event. Bob Colvin, president of the track,
solved the problem by renaming the event: "The 12th Renewal of
the Southern 500." Weatherly raced.

David Pearson hated the number thirteen and black cats.
Wilson recalled that Pearson once drove 25 miles out of his way
to get to the Charlotte track because a black cat had run across the
road in front of him. Pearson also shared a superstitious fear with
Dale Earnhardt: Both men hated peanuts in the pits. "I've seen
[Pearson] become livid about someone bringing peanuts in the

garage," Wilson said. This gooberous superstition greatly amused Earnhardt's best friend, Neil Bonnett, who always seemed to have peanuts when he was around Earnhardt.

For many years -- though exactly why seems to be a matter of great dispute -- green cars were taboo in NASCAR.

Despite Pearson's fears, black cats are right pretty. A medium is a steak. A key chain with a rabbit's foot wasn't too lucky for the rabbit. And what in the world is a blarney stone? About as superstitious as you get is to say "God bless you" when somebody sneezes.

You look indulgently upon good-luck charms, tarot cards, astrology, palm readers, and the like; they're really just amusing and harmless. So what's the problem? Nothing as long as you conduct yourself with the belief that superstitious objects and rituals – from broken mirrors to your daily horoscope – can't bring about good or bad luck. You aren't willing to let such notions and nonsense rule your life.

The danger of superstition lies in its ability to lure you into trusting it, thus allowing it some degree of influence over your life. In that case, it subverts God's rightful place.

Whether or not it's superstition, something does rule your life. It should be God – and God alone.

Most of the drivers decades ago were nuts when it came to being superstitious.

-- Waddell Wilson

Superstitions may not rule your life, but something does; it should be God and God alone.

THE BIG TIME

Read Matthew 2:19-23.

"He went and lived in a town called Nazareth" (v. 23).

It's a long way -- literally and figuratively -- from the dirt roads of Dawsonville, Ga., to the glitz of the Grand Ballroom at the Waldorf-Astoria Hotel in New York City, but Bill Elliott made the trip.

Tom Higgins called Elliott's odyssey an "incredible, 'Only-in-America' journey." It began in 1976 in an abandoned elementary schoolhouse in Dahlonega, Ga., in the north Georgia mountains. Elliott's dad had rented it for his sons to use because it was cheap and close to Dawsonville, their hometown.

"We had dreams back then, of course, like all young racers do," Elliott remembered. "But to think about coming to New York in the capacity as champions? Why, we might as well have thought about going to Mars. It seemed light-years away for us."

And yet, twelve years later, there he was in the limelight of New York City being honored as NASCAR's Winston Cup Series champion and conceding that he might be the most incongruous champion of NASCAR's modern era. "It's simply hard to imagine that we did it," said the man who was once described as "looking like Huckleberry Finn and sounding like Gomer Pyle" but who was such a fan favorite he was voted the most popular driver 16 times until he removed his name for consideration.

Awesome Bill from Dawsonville gave up racing fulltime after

NASCAR

the 2003 season and a career that saw him notch 44 victories. He claimed the Winston Cup million-dollar bonus in 1985 by winning the Daytona 500, the May race at Talladega, and the Southern 500 at Darlington. He literally rode from the backwoods to the big time. "It has been a long road," he said once with a sigh.

The move to the big time is one we often desire to make in our own lives. Bumps in the road, one stoplight communities, and towns with only a service station, a church, and a voting place litter the American countryside. Maybe you were born in one of them and grew up in a virtually unknown village in a backwater county. Perhaps you started out on a stage far removed from the bright lights of Broadway, the glitz of Hollywood, or the halls of power in Washington, D.C.

Those original circumstances don't have to define or limit you, though, for life is much more than geography as Bill Elliott's career demonstrates. It is about character and walking with God whether you're in the countryside or the city.

Jesus knew the truth of that. After all, he grew up in a small town in an inconsequential region of an insignificant country ruled by foreign invaders.

Where you are doesn't matter. What you are does.

Lordy, who would have ever thought it would come to this?
-- Bill Elliott in New York City being honored as NASCAR
Cup champion

**Where you live may largely be
the culmination of a series of circumstances;
what you are is a choice you make.**

DAY 6

STILL THE SAME

Read Hebrews 13:5-16.

"Jesus Christ is the same yesterday and today and forever" (v. 8).

Chevrolet. Dodge. Ford. And Toyota.

That last one is what got many NASCAR fans upset in 2007 when Toyota -- the face of the Japanese automobile industry -- showed up as the fourth manufacturer in the Nextel Cup series. And that, legions of fans decreed, was a slap at NASCAR tradition.

Not really, though.

Steven Cole Smith pointed out in an article about NASCAR tradition that as far back as 1953 NASCAR wasn't all-American. On June 21, 1953, six Jaguars, two Porsches, a Volkswagen, and an Aston Martin competed in the International 200 at Langhorne, Penn., on an oval dirt track. The foreign cars all finished, and a Jaguar driven by Dick Allwine came in sixth.

On June 13, 1954, at NASCAR's first-ever road race in Linden, N.J., Lee Petty in a Dodge, Buck Baker in an Oldsmobile, and Herb Thomas and Dick Rathmann in a pair of Hudsons were in the field. The race was won, however, by a Jaguar. Other brands included in the forty-three-car field were Austin-Healey, MG, Porsche, and Morgan.

In the 1958 Crown America 500 at Riverside, a pair of Citroens finished ahead of a Ford driven by Parnelli Jones, who did at least have the satisfaction of trouncing a Renault.

Toyota didn't exactly appear out of nowhere. The manufacturer raced in the now-defunct Goody's Dash series and then moved on to the Craftsman truck series before moving up to Cup competition. The appearance of a foreign manufacturer was actually a change back to the way things used to be.

Like everything else, NASCAR has changed. PCs and CDs, cell phones and George Foreman grills, iPods and IMAX theaters – they and much that is in your life now may not have even been around when you were 16. Think about how style, cars, communications, and tax laws constantly change.

Don't be too harsh on the world, though, because you've changed also. You've aged, gained or lost weight, gotten married, changed jobs, or relocated.

Have you ever found yourself bewildered by the rapid pace of change, casting about for something to hold on to that will always be the same, that you can use as an anchor for your life? Is there anything like that?

Sadly, the answer's no. All the things of this world change.

On the other hand, there's Jesus, who is the same today, the same forever, always dependable, always loving you. No matter what happens in your life, Jesus is still the same.

When I came along, I would have said you're crazy that we would be racing Toyotas one day.

-- Ricky Rudd

**In our ever-changing and bewildering world,
Jesus is the same forever;
his love for you will never change.**

THE PETTY WAY

Read Romans 13:8-14.

"The night is nearly over; the day is almost here. So let us put aside the deeds of darkness and put on the armor of light" (v. 12).

When Robin Pemberton went to work for Petty Enterprises, he learned there were three ways to do things: the right way, the wrong way, and the Petty way, "which was above and beyond."

Pemberton was appointed NASCAR's Vice President of Competition in 2004, but his fame came from his seventeen years as a crew chief for Rusty Wallace, Mark Martin, and Kyle Petty. He got his start as a mechanic and fabricator for the King after moving to North Carolina in 1979 with fifty bucks and a 1966 Corvette.

Pemberton believed his chance with the Pettys came about because of his dad's restaurant. Malta, N.Y., where Pemberton grew up, had a local racetrack, and his dad's place was on the route to the track. When the Winston Cup series came to Malta in 1971, young Pemberton met some of the Petty family when they stopped by to eat. Richard Petty "remembered the group of kids who were hanging around while they were working on their cars during those hot, summer days," Pemberton said. "So he made the connection, and more than likely I got the opportunity based on that."

"When I arrived," Pemberton said, "Richard was very much the King." The young mechanic quickly learned that things were different in the Petty camp. They taught him "you don't always win, but what's most important is how you carry it off when you lose, to always look good and be professional and behave."

The Petty way meant cars that were nicer than anybody else's, presentations that were better than everyone else's, and nicer uniforms. As Pemberton put it, the Petty team understood "there is more to it than the immediate goal of winning the race."

Like Richard Petty and his team, you have a way of life that defines and describes you. You're a die-hard NASCAR fan for starters. Maybe you're married with a family. A city guy or a small-town gal. You wear jeans or a suit to work every day. And then there's your faith.

For the Christian, following Jesus more than anything else defines for the world your way of life. It's basically simple in its concept even if it is downright daunting in its execution. You act toward others in a way that would not embarrass you were your day to be broadcast on Fox News. You think about others in a way that would not humiliate you should your thoughts be the plot line for a new CBS sitcom.

You make your actions and thoughts those of love: at all times, in all things, toward all people. It's the Jesus way of life, and it's the way to life forever with God.

The Petty way taught you to represent something bigger than yourself or the company.

-- Robin Pemberton

To follow Jesus is to act with love at all times, in all things, and toward all people.

FRUIT TREES

Read Matthew 7:15-20.

"By their fruit you will recognize them" (v. 20).

The first person to reach Buck Baker's crashed car saw such carnage that he reported Baker had been decapitated -- but Baker wasn't hurt at all.

In 1998, Elzie Wylie Baker, Sr. was named one of NASCAR's fifty greatest drivers. In 1956 and '57, he became the first driver to win back-to-back championships. In all, he won 46 races, including the Southern 500 at Darlington three times. He finished in the top ten 372 times. Baker was inducted into the International Motorsports Hall of Fame in 1990 and the Motorsports Hall of Fame of America in 1998.

It was in 1950 at the first running of the Southern 500 that an uninjured Baker was presumed dead. The race marked the first 500-mile race ever for stock cars. Many experts figured that neither the cars nor the drivers would last 500 miles because of the oppressive heat and humidity of a Labor-Day weekend in the South Carolina low country. The drivers were determined to prove the "experts" wrong.

When Baker wrecked, the first person on the scene "looked inside and recoiled in horror. 'No need to bother with Baker,' he said. 'The poor guy has had his head cut off.'"

That shaken and shocked person had based his assessment of the situation on the blood that was all over the car and the driver

-- but he was mistaken. Most drivers had taken something cold to drink with them in their cars to help them weather the heat. Baker's choice was a gallon jug of cold tomato juice. Other than being covered with tomato juice -- and not blood -- Baker was unhurt.

Strawberry shortcake. Apple pie. Ice-cold watermelon. Banana pudding. Straight up, congealed, or served with whipped cream or ice cream, fresh fruit is hard to beat. We even use it symbolically to represent the good things in our lives: A promotion or a raise is the fruit of our good work.

Fruity metaphors and images conjure up thoughts of something sweet and satisfying. Little in life, however, is as rancid as fruit gone bad. That dual image of fruit at its best and its worst is what Jesus had in mind when he spoke of knowing both false prophets and faithful followers by their fruit.

Our lives as disciples of Jesus should yield not just material fruits but spiritual fruits also. Our spiritual fruits are what we leave in our wake: heartbreak, tears, anger, bitterness, and dissension; or peace, love, joy, generosity, and gentleness.

Good or bad – delicious or rotten -- these are the fruits by which we shall be known by those around us. More importantly, they are the fruits by which God knows us.

Wonder if they have boiled peanuts in California.
-- Ken Schrader when he heard California Speedway was getting Darlington's Labor Day weekend date

God knows you by your spiritual fruits,
not the material ones the world fancies so.

FORGIVE AND FORGET

Mark 11:22-25.

*"If you hold anything against anyone, forgive him, so that
your Father in heaven may forgive you your sins" (v. 25).*

A professed Christian, Darrell Waltrip once learned a lesson
about the power of forgiveness.

Waltrip wasn't in a forgiving mood after Ricky Craven knocked
his car out of a race at North Carolina Speedway in Rockingham. "I was livid, fit to be tied," Waltrip recalled, and he tore
after Craven. "I ran into the garage and snatched Ricky's window
net down. I was just about to get into it with him." Waltrip fully
intended to crawl right into Craven's car until some of his crew
members dragged him away.

Waiting for him was Max Helton, the NASCAR chaplain who
had helped Waltrip and others found Motor Racing Outreach in
1988. Helton's message was blunt: Darrell, you're being a lousy
witness and you need to think about what you're doing.

Waltrip responded to Helton that he couldn't let it go, that
he was "going back over there right now and have this out with
Ricky." Helton then stood in the doorway and said, "Here, Darrell,
take it out on me. Hit me instead. This will save you from making
a big mistake." The ludicrousness of the idea broke Waltrip's
anger and he laughed.

The next week at Phoenix, Helton asked Waltrip to pray at the
chapel service after the drivers' meeting. He went to the front of

the room, and Craven was sitting on the front row. Waltrip found he couldn't pray because of the guilt he still bore over his anger the week before. He told the group, "I have something to take care of" before he could pray. He called Craven up front, put his arm around him, and asked him for forgiveness. "Then I prayed."

Remember that buddy you used to go fishing with? That friend you used to roam the mall with? The one who introduced you to sushi? Remember that person who was so special you thought this might be "the one"? And now you don't even speak because of something -- who remembers exactly? -- one of you did.

Fractured relationships are as much a part of life as sunshine and aching feet. In discussing the matter of people we greet coldly if at all, Jesus' instructions were simple: forgive the other person. Admittedly, this is easier said than done for everybody except Jesus, but reconciling with others sets you free to get on with your life. Harboring a grudge is a way to self-destruction; kissing and making up is a way to inner peace and contentment.

Forgiveness, thus, is another of God's gifts to help us toward richer, fuller lives. Besides, you can never outforgive God, who forgives you.

I don't know why they settle this stuff on the racetrack. I guess they're too scared to settle it outside the racetrack.

-- *Jeremy Mayfield*

Making up with others frees
you from your past, turning you loose
to get on with your richer, fuller future.

OLD TIMERS

Read Psalm 92.

*"[The righteous] will still bear fruit in old age, they will
stay fresh and green, proclaiming, 'The Lord is upright'"
(vv. 14-15).*

In 1989, when Dick Trickle was named NASCAR's Rookie of the
Year, he was 48 years old and a two-time grandfather.

Trickle always did things his way. For instance, he drove in
cowboy boots -- snakeskin, of course. One time, though, a new
pair of his boots wasn't properly broken in. When the floorboard
heated them up, they put the squeeze on his feet. In pain, Trickle
radioed in to his crew to get him some "regular" driving shoes
ready. When he pitted, crew members dived headlong into his car
to wrestle with his swollen feet and the hot boots.

Trickle also drilled a hole in his safety helmet and installed
cigarette lighters in his cars so he could smoke while racing. In
the 1990 Winston 500 (appropriately enough), the in-car camera
caught him lighting up and smoking as he raced.

Despite being the oldest Rookie of the Year in NASCAR history,
Trickle was considered "possibly the most experienced stock car
driver in racing." He had 31 years of racing and more than 1,200
wins behind him. But what took him so long to step up to the big
time? Simple. He always did so well on the Midwest stock-car
racing circuit that he was never really very interested in doing
anything else. Only when the Stavola Brothers lost a driver right

before Rockingham and called Trickle did he head South.

How did he manage to stay so young in such a grinding, dangerous sport? He was never seriously hurt. "Someone asked me what it felt like to be a 48-year-old rookie," he said. "I couldn't tell them because I knew what it felt like to be a rookie, but not 48. The trick to life is feeling good."

Even if we don't always feel as young as ageless wonder Dick Trickle managed to, we don't like to admit – even to ourselves – that we're not as young as we used to be. After all, we live in a youth-obsessed culture.

So we keep plastic surgeons in business, dye our hair, buy cases of those miracle wrinkle-reducing creams, suck in our stomachs at the beach, and redouble our efforts in the gym. Sometimes, though, we just have to face up to the truth the mirror tells us: We're getting older every day.

It's really all right, though, because aging and old age are part of the natural cycle of our lives, which was God's idea in the first place. God's conception of the golden years, though, doesn't include unlimited close encounters with a rocking chair and nothing more.

God expects us to serve him as we are able all the days of our life. Those who serve God flourish no matter their age because the energizing power of God is in them.

The car doesn't know how old you are.

-- *Ken Schrader*

**Servants of God don't ever retire; they keep
working until they get the ultimate promotion.**

TEARS IN HEAVEN

Read Revelation 21:1-8.

*"[God] will wipe every tear from their eyes. There will be
no more death or mourning or crying or pain" (v. 4).*

A touched and touching Neil Bonnett once brought everyone
to tears in a post-race interview.

In February 1988 NASCAR sanctioned an exhibition race in
Australia in which Bonnett raced to a dramatic victory, finishing
.86 seconds ahead of Bobby Allison. The win continued Bonnett's
comeback from a horrific wreck the previous October at Charlotte
Motor Speedway that had crushed his right leg and jeopardized
his career.

In his interview, Bonnett couldn't hold back his tears as he spoke
of the tears he had shed because of both the long-term outlook
for his recovery and the pain of the therapy he had undergone
in the wake of the crash. "Not many people know how bad that
wreck really was," he said. The days immediately after the wreck
"were the worst I've ever known. The people were wonderful, but
the prognosis was that I was going to lose my leg. I was crying. I
was really low. Then Bobby [Allison] came by. . . . He said, 'You
can't give up. I won't let you give up.'"

Bonnett went on to note what a strange hand life sometimes
deals in that Allison and he had just finished racing head-to-head
for the first NASCAR victory in Australia. With everyone in tears,
an Aussie fan who had seen his first race ever perhaps spoke

for everyone: "Richard Petty and Dale Earnhardt are the Yank drivers we'd really like to see. For now, though, our hearts belong to Neil Bonnett."

On Feb. 11, 1994, those who loved Bonnett were again brought to tears when he was killed while practicing for the Daytona 500. He was 47.

When your parents died. When a friend told you she was divorcing. When you broke your collarbone. When you watch a sad movie.

You cry. Crying is as much a part of life as are hamburgers, bad television shows, and indigestion. Usually our tears are brought on by pain, sorrow, or disappointment.

But what about when your child was born? When your favorite driver won the Daytona 500? When you discovered Jesus Christ? Those times elicit tears too; we cry at the times of our greatest, most overwhelming joy.

Thus, while there will be tears in Heaven, they will only be tears of sheer, unmitigated, undiluted joy. The greatest joy possible, a joy beyond our imagining, must occur when we finally see Christ. If we shed tears of joy or excitement when we meet a NASCAR driver face-to-face, can we really believe that we will stand dry-eyed and calm in the presence of Jesus?

What we will not shed in Heaven are tears of sorrow and pain.

If I cry, it means I'm too weak to compete in this sport. That's bull.
-- Shawna Robinson

Tears in Heaven will be like everything else there:
a part of the joy we will experience.

TOUGH COOKIES

Read 2 Corinthians 11:21b-29.

"Besides everything else, I face daily the pressure of my concern for all the churches" (v. 28).

Paul "Little Bud" Moore knew one thing for sure about his fellow drivers: They were the "toughest breed of people I have seen in my entire life."

Moore began racing in the Grand National Series in 1964. His best season in the point standings was in 1968 when he finished 29th. He retired in 1973 without a win but with enough memories to last a lifetime.

He got the racing bug as a youngster in Charleston. His "dad had an old plumbing truck with scaffolding, and he took all the kids, and we'd get on top" and go to the races. As a result, Moore never wanted to be anything but a dirt track racer.

When he made it to the big time, he found himself slightly awed. "Early on I can remember looking at these drivers and thinking, how tough can you get?"

How did he survive in such a rough-and-tumble profession? He had an excellent tutor: Ralph Earnhardt. "He made me mean," Moore remembered. "He taught you how to convince a lot of the other competitors that you were tough enough to be left alone. He had ways, when you went to the track, you already had a lot of people whipped before the race even started."

Earnhardt wasn't the only tough cookie around. For instance,

NASCAR

Tiny Lund "was probably as tough an individual as I ever met in my life. . . . Didn't come no tougher than him."

And it wasn't just the drivers who were tough and mean in that era. At the Greenville-Pickens track, Moore remembered, he couldn't back up against the pit fence "because the women would cut you with a knife."

You don't have to be a NASCAR driver to be tough. In America today, toughness isn't restricted to physical accomplishments and brute strength. Going to work every morning even when you feel bad, sticking by your rules for your children in a society that ridicules parental authority, making hard decisions about your aging parents' care often over their objections — you've got to be tough every day just to live honorably, decently, and justly.

Living faithfully requires toughness, too, though in America chances are you won't be imprisoned, stoned, or flogged this week for your faith as Paul was. Still, contemporary society exerts subtle, psychological, daily pressures on you to turn your back on your faith and your values. Popular culture promotes promiscuity, atheism, and gutter language; your children's schools have kicked God out; the corporate culture advocates amorality before the shrine of the almighty dollar.

You have to hang tough to keep the faith.

The people in that era were very tough. Today, they just throw water bottles where they used to come across with a tire iron.

-- Paul "Little Bud" Moore

**Life demands more than mere physical toughness;
you must be spiritually tough too.**

THE BAD TIMES

Read Philippians 1:3-14.

*"What has happened to me has really served to advance
the gospel. . . . Most of the brothers in the Lord have been
encouraged to speak the word of God more courageously
and fearlessly" (vv. 12, 14).*

Curtis Ross Turner, the son of NASCAR's Curtis Turner, knew
bad times, but he also found where to go for the good times.

Curtis Turner won more than three hundred races in a career
that began in the 1940s and ended with his death. He was "the
brains behind the Charlotte Motor Speedway," but he ran into
trouble when the cost of the track escalated beyond his ability to
pay for it. Turner desperately attempted to unionize the drivers to
get an $800,000 loan from the Teamsters Union to finish the track.
Bill France responded by banning him from NASCAR for life in
1961. Until then, Ross Turner had a childhood he remembered as
"a whirlwind of fun and adventure." That was over.

Turner went bankrupt, losing his interest in the track. He barely
had enough money to feed his family, and they began moving
from house to house, leaving when the rent came due.

In October 1970, Curtis Turner was killed in a plane crash.
Ross Turner was 15, and though his dad had been reinstated
by NASCAR in 1965, his schizophrenic mother, his sister, and
he "didn't even get grocery money" out of his father's estate. "It
was so bad that on a couple of occasions my younger sister and

I actually stole bread and milk from a convenience store just to bring something into the house," Turner recalled.

His sister and he became wards of the state and were placed in an orphanage when their mother was institutionalized for treatment. Right there in the worst of times, 17-year-old Ross Turner found what he needed to take him to the best of times. He found Jesus Christ and eventually went into the ministry.

Loved ones die. You're downsized. Your biopsy looks cancerous. Your spouse could be having an affair. Hard, tragic times are as much a part of life as breath.

This applies to Christians too. Christianity is not the equivalent of a Get-out-of-Jail-Free card, granting us a lifelong exemption from either the least or the worst pain the world has to offer. While Jesus promises us he will be there to lead us through the valleys, he never promises that we will not enter them.

The question therefore becomes how you handle the bad times. You can buckle to your knees in despair and cry, "Why me?" Or you can hit your knees in prayer and ask, "What do I do with this?"

Setbacks and tragedies are opportunities to reveal and to develop true character and abiding faith. Your faithfulness -- not your skipping merrily along through life without pain -- is what reveals the depth of your love for God.

Tough times are the Lord's way of teaching me to be strong.
-- Geoffrey Bodine

Faithfulness to God requires faith even in --
especially in -- the hard times.

SOUTHERN HOSPITALITY

Read 2 Kings 4:8-17.

*"Let's make a small room on the roof and put in it a bed
and a table, a chair and a lamp for him. Then he can stay
there whenever he comes to us" (v. 10).*

Junior Johnson's momma took Southern hospitality to a new
level when she served coffee and pie to the men who were trying
to put her family in prison.

The Junior Johnson legend has its roots in the family
moonshining business in Wilkes County, N.C. As one of Johnson's
friends put it, "If you wanted to have a little money in your pocket,
you had to mess with moonshine. It was a way of life for us" in a
place and an age when supporting a family was difficult.

Junior dropped out of school in the mid 1940s to help out. "It
was hard, dangerous and scary work," he once said. "It was how
we made our living back then. That's all. It ain't nothing to be
ashamed of. Makin' moonshine was a hand-me-down trade that
was passed down through the generations where I came from."

Hauling moonshine was also how Johnson honed his driving
skills, outrunning and outsmarting the revenuers. He became an
expert on figuring out how to get a little extra power out of his
cars so he could leave his pursuers eating dust.

His family lived in constant fear of the law. Junior saw his father
repeatedly hauled off to jail for running illegal liquor; the senior
Johnson would ultimately spend nearly twenty years in prison.

Junior's mother, Lara Belle, made the most of a tough situation. "Their house was raided so often that she occasionally offered the visiting revenuers a cup of coffee and perhaps a piece of pie as they took a break from hauling out stashes of illegal liquor."

As Junior Johnson's mother illustrated, Southerners are deservedly famous for their hospitality. Down South, warmth and genuineness seem genetic. You open your home to the neighborhood kids, to your friends, to the stranger whose car broke down in the rain, to the stray cat that showed up hungry and hollering. You even let family members overstay their welcome without grumbling.

Hospitality was vital to the cultures of Biblical times also. Travelers faced innumerable dangers: everything from lions to bandits to deadly desert heat. Finding a temporary haven thus often became quite literally a matter of life and death.

Since hospitality has through the ages been a sign of a loving and generous nature, it is not surprising that almighty God himself is a gracious host. He welcomes you, not as a stranger, but as an adopted child. One glorious day this hospitable God will open the doors of his place for you -- and never ask you to leave.

The NASCAR Nextel Cup Series used to always take the weekend of Mother's Day off in the spirit of true Southern hospitality. There was no excuse why anyone affiliated with NASCAR wouldn't be with their mother.

--Micah Roberts, VegasInsider.com

Hospitality is an outward sign of the inward loving, generous, and godly nature of the host.

LEVELHEADED

Read Romans 3:21-26.

"There is no distinction, since all have sinned and fall short of the glory of God" (vv. 22b-23 NRSV).

NASCAR's version of a level playing field has cost Jeff Gordon the championship at least twice.

Richard Petty and Dale Earnhardt both won seven Cup titles in their storied careers. Gordon won four titles early in his career: 1995, 1997, 1998, and 2001. He very well could have had two more had not NASCAR tinkered with the numbers.

As is well known, drivers accumulate points through the season to determine who makes it into the ten-race, season-ending chase for the championship. It's exciting all right. But when the regular season ends, NASCAR resets the points. The drivers basically start over.

Had not NASCAR leveled the playing field for the championship chase, Gordon in 2007 would have won the Cup title before the final race of the season was even run. He would also have been the champion in 2004.

How does Gordon feel about a format designed to level the playing field that has worked to his disadvantage? "I don't think anything is unfair when you know going into it what it is," he said diplomatically. "We know what we've got to do. The points are whatever NASCAR decides to make it, and we're going to race the championship however they do it."

Gordon's lone concern about the changes is how they affect NASCAR's storied history. He noted that comparing champions before the Chase to champions after the Chase began is difficult if not impossible. "It's very hard to create new history for the sport when they change it like that," he said.

History has clearly shown that the rule changes that leveled the playing field provided a boost to the title for Jimmie Johnson in 2007 and Kurt Busch in 2004.

We should face up to one of life's basic facts: Its playing field isn't level. Others, it seems, get all the breaks. They get the cushy job; they win the lottery; their father owns the business. Some people – perhaps undeservedly -- just have it made.

That said, we just have to accept that the playing field isn't level and get over it. Dwelling on life's inequities can create only bitterness and cynicism, leading us to grumble about what we don't have while ignoring the blessings God continuously showers upon us. A moment's pause and reflection is all it takes for us to call to mind any number of friends, acquaintances, and strangers with whom we would not exchange situations.

The only place in life where we really stand on a level playing field is before God. There, all people are equal because we all need the lifeline God offers through Jesus and we all have access to it.

As long as it's the same for everybody, and as long as the guy with the most points wins, the theory is still the same.
*   -- Tony Stewart on rule changes made to the chase in 2007*

Unlike life's playing field, God's playing field
is level because everyone has equal access
to what God has done through Jesus Christ.

THE BEAUTIFUL PEOPLE

Read Matthew 23:23-28.

"Woe to you, teachers of the law and Pharisees, you hypocrites! You are like whitewashed tombs, which look beautiful on the outside, but on the inside are full of dead men's bones and everything unclean" (v. 27).

Judy Judge was one of the beautiful people, part of the cream of Daytona Beach society. Racing and racers were not part of her world -- until she met some guy named Bobby.

Judge grew up loved, pampered, and privileged, a high-school cheerleader who went to college. She knew about racing and racers but said, "Nice girls in Daytona did not do that. We were not part of that crowd."

That all changed for her, though, in 1958 when she was 21 and she met a handsome older man at a dance club. He told her his name was Bobby Edwards. "He was a good dancer, fun to dance with," she recalled. For six months she met him regularly and they just danced.

In February 1959, a college friend prodded her into attending a race. Her father granted her permission to go, "as long as you behave yourself." At the race, she bought a program and learned the truth: Her dancing friend was Glenn "Fireball" Roberts. "I was very shocked," Judge said. "I was *real* shocked. I couldn't believe what I was seeing."

But she met him at the dance club after the race, and during "a long conversation" "Bobby Edwards" explained: He had realized that if she had known who he really was then she wouldn't have had anything to do with him. She told him he was right.

She saw him race one more time, and "I was hooked. That was it." One of the beautiful people had found her true love where she least expected it: at the race track.

Remember the brunette who sat behind you in history class? Or the blonde in English? And how about that hunk from the next apartment who washes his car every Saturday morning and just forces you to get outside earlier than you really want to?

We do love those beautiful people.

It is worth remembering amid our adulation of superficial beauty that *Vogue* or *People* probably wouldn't have been too enamored of Jesus' looks. Isaiah 53 declares that our savior "had no beauty or majesty to attract us to him, nothing in his appearance that we should desire him."

Though Jesus never urged folks to walk around with body odor and unwashed hair, he did admonish us to avoid being overly concerned with physical beauty, which fades with age despite tucks and Botox. What matters to God is inner beauty, which reveals itself in the practice of justice, mercy, and faith, and which is not only lifelong but eternal.

I knew he loved me when he bought me waders for Christmas.
-- Judy Judge on Fireball Roberts

**When it comes to looking good to God,
it's what's inside that counts.**

AT A LOSS

Read Philippians 3:7-11.

"I consider everything a loss compared to the surpassing greatness of knowing Christ Jesus my Lord, for whose sake I have lost all things" (v. 8).

The death of a family member is a painful loss, but how much worse is the pain if the family isn't sure the loved one is dead?

Mario Rossi had a long and distinguished NASCAR career as a mechanic, engine builder, crew chief, and car owner. He built a reputation as an innovator and an engine wizard. His sister recalled that by the time he was nine he could take a tractor apart and put it together in tip-top running condition.

His relationship with NASCAR was described as "a rocky one," and as early as 1971 he spoke of retiring. His last position in NASCAR was as team manager for DiGard Racing for which he signed a young driver named Darrell Waltrip in 1975. Shortly thereafter, he left NASCAR for good.

In 1982, he boarded a plane in Philadelphia after spending Christmas with his family. Two days later came word that Rossi had died in a plane crash off the coast of the Bahamas. His remains were never recovered, and the family grew suspicious of the story of the crash. They learned that the plane Rossi was piloting and died in had been resold three times since its "crash." To their inquiries for information about Rossi's placement in a Witness Protection Program, the family received only a terse reply: "The

Marshals Service will neither confirm nor deny the existence of the records you seek."

His sister wouldn't give up: "It has been more than twenty years of total frustration," she once said, "not knowing if Mario is alive or dead. We, as a family, must have closure."

The pain of their loss was fresh every day.

Maybe, as it was with the Rossi family, it was when a family member died. Perhaps it wasn't so staggeringly tragic: your puppy died, your best friend moved away, or an older sibling left home. Sometime in your youth or early adult life, though, you learned that loss is a part of life.

Loss inevitably diminishes your life, but loss and the grief that accompanies it are part of the price of loving. When you first encountered loss, you learned that you were virtually helpless to prevent it or escape it.

There is life after loss, though, because you have one sure place to turn. Jesus can share your pain and ease your suffering, but he doesn't stop there. Through the loss of his own life, he has transformed death -- the ultimate loss -- into the ultimate gain of eternal life. In Jesus lies the promise that one day loss itself will die.

Nothing we do can bring back those that we've lost as part of our sport. We can, however, learn from those losses and honor them in what we do moving forward
-- NASCAR President Mike Helton, addressing safety issues

Jesus not only eases the pain of our losses
but transforms the loss caused by death
into the gain of eternal life.

THE GOOD OLD DAYS

Read Psalm 102.

"My days vanish like smoke; . . . but you remain the same,
and your years will never end" (vv. 3, 27).

Once upon a time a driver could enter a race with a rental car. Frank Mundy did it.

Mundy drove a 1949 Cadillac in NASCAR's first-ever race on June 19, 1949, in Charlotte. He was in the lead when a right wheel fell off. "The cars were literally stock off the showroom floor, and the spindles weren't strong enough to take the pressure during turns at such high speeds."

In April 1951, Mundy towed a Nash to Gardena, California, for the race there, driving straight through from Atlanta and taking about a day and a half for the trip. When he arrived, though, the Nash company told him he couldn't race his car because it would not be introduced to the public until the following week.

Mundy was on his way to the track anyway race day, riding with Bill France, the godfather of NASCAR, when they passed a rental car lot. Mundy said, "I came all this distance, and I went over and rented a Plymouth coupe. France didn't say a thing. He probably figured I was crazy, but we had come too far not to race."

Mundy found some whitewash that was used to paint curbs, painted an X on the car and, "went to the track where I got a seat-belt and strapped the doors. I entered the race with my rental car and stayed out of everybody's way." Memories of the right wheel falling off at Charlotte meant Mundy avoided going hard into the turns to keep the pressure off the tires. He finished 11th out of 20, won \$25, and flew home on France's private plane.

Those "good old days" are gone forever, though. The NASCAR Frank Mundy knew and the atmosphere in which he raced no longer exist. Times change.

It's a brutal truth that time just never stands still. The current of your life sweeps you along until you realize one day you've lived long enough to have a past. Part of it you cling to fondly. The stunts you pulled with your high-school buddies. Your first apartment. That dance with your first love. That special vacation. Those "good old days."

You hold on relentlessly to the memory of those old, familiar ways because of the stability they provide in our uncertain world. They will always be there even as times change and you age.

Another constant exists in your life too. God has been a part of every event in your life that created a memory because he was there. He's always there with you; the question is whether you ignore him or make him a part of your day.

A "good old day" is any day shared with God.

Years ago, you used to get out and fight and run around and chase each other with a jackhammer and stuff like that. Those were the good old days.
--Dale Earnhardt, Jr. on NASCAR track etiquette

Today is one of the "good old days"
if you share it with God.

THE INTERVIEW

Read Romans 14: 1-12.

"We will all stand before God's judgment seat. . . . So then, each of us will give an account of himself to God" (vv. 10, 12).

Lou LaRosa probably needed to sharpen up his interview skills before he walked into the shop of the DiGard race team in the late 1960s looking for a job. He wound up working for nothing -- and it was his idea.

LaRosa is one of NASCAR's legendary engine builders. He won the "NASCAR Engine Builder of the Year" award in 1987. Dale Earnhardt, David Pearson, Cale Yarborough, Ricky Rudd, and Brett Bodine are among the drivers who have driven LaRosa's powerful engines to victory.

He grew up in Brooklyn, not exactly a NASCAR hotbed, but early on he was fascinated by engines. After high school, he worked at a bank during the day and at a gas station as a mechanic at night. He did that for two years before quitting the bank and concentrating on the cars.

LaRosa raced briefly on Long Island after a stint in Viet Nam but was basically unemployed when an acquaintance told him the DiGard race team in Daytona Beach was looking for help. So he drove down to Daytona, sauntered into the shop office, and told the receptionist he wanted a job application.

She wasn't too encouraging. She said, "'You can fill one out, but we have a stack this tall,' putting her hands about a foot apart." While LaRosa pondered that setback, Jim Gardner, the owner's brother came in, and LaRosa had a brainstorm. He told him, "I'll work for you for nothing for a month, and if you like it, you hire me, and if you don't, that's fine." Gardner liked the bizarre idea, a deal was struck, and a career was launched.

You know all about job interviews even if you've never had one in which you offered to work for nothing. You've experienced the stress, the anxiety, the helpless feeling. You tried to appear calm and relaxed, struggling to come up with reasonably original answers to banal questions and to cover up the fact that you thought the interviewer was a total geek. You told yourself that if they turned you down, it was their loss, not yours.

You won't be so indifferent, though, about your last interview: the one with God. A day will come when we will all stand before God to account for ourselves. It is to God and God alone – not our friends, not our parents, not society in general – that we must give a final and complete account.

Since all eternity will be at stake, it sure would help to have a character witness with you. One – and only one -- is available: Jesus Christ.

"What do you want to do?" "Build engines." "You ain't ever going to make it."
-- *Lou LaRosa's first conversation with the great engine builder*
Robert Gee

You will have one last interview -- with God --
and you sure want Jesus there to vouch for you.

DAY 20

RAIN CHECK

Read Genesis 9:8-17.

"I establish my covenant with you: Never again will all life be cut off by the waters of a flood; never again will there be a flood to destroy the earth" (v. 11).

Even the threat of rain can play a part in the outcome of a race.

When Davey Allison and his crew showed up in Darlington for the Southern 500 on Labor Day weekend of 1992, they had a chance to become the first team since Bill Elliott's in 1985 to win the Winston Million, a $1 million bonus awarded for winning any three of the Daytona 500, the Winston 500 at Talladega, the Coca-Cola 600 at Charlotte, and the Southern 500.

So Allison's crew chief, Larry McReynolds, did everything he could to give his driver an edge "including affixing Allison's No. 28 upside down on the roof as Elliott had accidentally done in 1985). Allison was in contention as the final 100 miles approached, but McReynolds anxiously watched the skies and faced a crucial decision. Allison's Ford needed fuel, but those skies were threatening rain. McReynolds knew that if rain cut the race short, his driver needed to stay on the track as long as he could.

McReynolds ordered one of his team members to hurry over to the NASCAR truck to check the weather radar. When the man returned he told his boss, "It looks good." McReynolds then ordered Allison to pit to get enough fuel to finish the race.

To McReynolds' dismay, only a few laps passed before the

rain started. NASCAR eventually chose not to restart the race. Darrell Waltrip, who had not pitted, was declared the winner. A thoroughly confused McReynolds tracked down his messenger and asked for an explanation, but the crew member also was at a loss. He had looked at the radar, and "there was green everywhere around us."

For him, of course, green meant go. On the radar, though, it meant rain.

The kids are on go for their picnic. Your golf game is set. You have rib eyes and smoked sausage ready for the grill when the gang comes over tonight. And then it rains.

Sometimes, unlike a NASCAR race, you can slog on through a downpour. Often, however, the rain simply washes away your carefully laid plans, and you can't do anything about it. Just as race day is at the mercy of the rain.

Rain falls when and where it wants to without checking with you. It answers only to God, the one who controls the heavens from which it comes, the ground on which it falls, and everything in between -- territory that should include you.

Though God has absolute dominance over the rain, he will take control of your life only if you let him. In daily seeking his will for your life, you discover that you can live so as to be walking in the sunshine even when it's raining.

Few things are worse than a NASCAR rain delay.
-- NASCAR Writer Monte Dutton

Into each life some rain must fall,
but you can live in the glorious light of God's love
even during a downpour.

NO GETTING OVER IT

Read Ephesians 2:1-10.

"It is by grace you have been saved, through faith -- and this not from yourselves, it is the gift of God -- not by works, so that no one can boast" (vv. 8-9).

Hill Overton, Jr. was thirteen when he climbed a tree and saw his first NASCAR race. He never got over it.

Overton spent most of fifty years as a broadcaster and track announcer. His love affair with NASCAR began on June 19, 1949, on a three-quarter-mile dirt track in Charlotte when Bill France held his first race for "strictly stock" cars. Overton ran in the local All-American Soapbox Derby competition, and the officials handed out T-shirts to the racers along with an admonition to go to France's race and wear the T-shirts.

Overton had to badger his dad into taking him since he had to drive across town. His dad relented, but they ran into such a massive traffic jam that by the time they arrived, the track was packed with an overflow crowd and they couldn't get in.

"We found a weeping willow tree on a high bank over turn three," Overton recalled. "There was just a board fence around the track in those days. We watched the race and ate dirt from up there, and that was my first real NASCAR exposure."

It was enough. "It was the sound . . . the noise . . . the dirt . . . the roar . . . the furor. It just embedded itself into me and I've been a racing nut ever since." Overton was hooked for life. After that first race, "there was not much that he would allow to come between him and his desire to be around racing."

Overton, who would work as the public address announcer at Darlington and Rockingham, drove "his parents nuts on trips by sitting in the backseat pretending to be broadcasting racing. I was the announcer who'd say, 'Here they go! Vrrroommm!' I'd do all that stuff."

Hill Overton, Jr. found that once you meet NASCAR, you never get over it.

Some things in life have a way of getting under your skin and never letting go. Your passion may have begun the first time you rode in a convertible. Or when your breath was taken away the first time you saw the one who would become your spouse. You knew you were hooked the first time you walked through the track gates on race day.

You can put God's love on that list, too. Once you encounter it in the person of Jesus Christ, you never get over it. That's because when you sincerely give your life to Jesus by acknowledging him as the Lord of your life, God's love – his grace – changes you. It sets you free to live in peace and in joy, free from the fear of death's apparent victory.

When you meet Jesus, you're never the same again. You just never get over the experience.

If it had anything to do with racing, I was into it. I wanted to go.
                                                                — *Hill Overton, Jr.*

**Some things hit you so hard you're never
the same again; meeting Jesus is like that.**

FLAT BROKE

Read Luke 16:1-15.

"You cannot serve both God and money" (v. 13b).

Dale Yarborough was once so broke he had to borrow thirteen cents from a toll-booth operator so he could get to a race.

Yarborough is a true NASCAR legend, Winston Cup champion for three straight years (1976-78), winner of 83 races including four at Daytona, and a member of the Motorsports Hall of Fame of America. In 1998, he was named one of NASCAR's 50 Greatest Drivers.

1964 was apparently not a very good year for turkeys in Timmonsville, S.C., and Yarborough was apparently a much better driver than he was a turkey farmer because he went through his life savings trying to raise a crop of the gobblers. When he was offered a car for a race in Savannah, Yarborough "cashed a check for his last $10, made two sandwiches with what he could scrounge out of the refrigerator, packed his wife Betty Jo into their car and headed south to Savannah."

On the way, though, he lost the $10 to a speeding ticket for driving 40 in a 35-mph zone. A major-league crisis arose when the young couple found themselves at a toll bridge; they needed 50 cents to cross -- and they were flat broke. Yarborough dug around in the cracks of the backseat "like a dog digging for a chipmunk" and managed to come up with 37 cents, but they were still short. "The presence of Yarborough's sobbing, hungry, pregnant, pretty young wife being fairly persuasive," the soft-hearted toll keeper yielded to his finer instincts, contributed the balance, and waved the couple through.

Yarborough made it to Savannah and promptly blew his engine while he was warming up. With no winnings and no money, he borrowed $20 from the race's promoter to get home, along the way paying the toll keeper the thirteen cents he had borrowed.

Having a little too much money at the end of the month may be as bothersome -- if not as worrisome -- as having a little too much month at the end of the money. The investment possibilities are bewildering: stocks, bonds, mutual funds, that group pooling their money to open up a neighborhood coffee shop -- that's a good idea.

You take your money seriously, as well you should. Jesus, too, took money seriously, warning us frequently of its dangers. Money itself is not evil; its peril lies in the ease with which it can usurp God's rightful place as the master of our lives.

Certainly in our age and society, we often measure people by how much money they have. But like our other talents, gifts, and resources, money should primarily be used for God's purposes. God's love must touch not only our hearts but our wallets also.

How much of your wealth are you investing with God?

One time Buck Baker, Lee Petty, and I had to put our money together just to split a hog dog and a Coke.
-- Louise Smith, NASCAR's first woman driver

**Your attitude about money says much
about your attitude toward God.**

DAY 23

LIMITED-TIME OFFER

Read Psalm 103.

"As for man, his days are like grass, he flourishes like a
flower of the field; the wind blows over it and it is gone.
. . . But from everlasting to everlasting the Lord's love is
with those who fear him" (vv. 15-17).

Adam Petty was only nineteen when he died on May 12, 2000, from head trauma suffered during a practice session in New Hampshire.

Several days after the accident, Adam's grandfather, Richard, the King, talked with the media about the incomprehensible loss. He confessed he wrestled with some guilt because he had introduced his grandson to the sport that had taken his life.

Adam Petty had shaken hands with death even before that fateful day in Loudon. On Sept. 7, 1998, he pulled in for a routine pit stop during a race at the Minnesota State Fairgrounds as part of the American Speed Association circuit, a proving ground for young drivers. His crew chief, Chris Bradley, 40, jumped under the car to adjust a sway bar apparently without informing anyone else of what he was doing. When the jack dropped after the tires had been changed, Adam did what all drivers are trained to do: He hit the pedal and got moving. Bradley was still under the car and was killed.

Adam turned to his grandfather for some consolation. In 1965 in Georgia, the King's dragster had soared into the crowd and

half-mile track, a lot of cars, scoring wasn't very good there," Makar remembered. "Somehow or other, they did something in the scoring where they said we were a lap down."

Race officials refused to award the victory to Waltrip, who in turn refused to give the victory trophy back. They kept their results and Waltrip kept their trophy.

Even the most modest and self-effacing among us can't help but be pleased by prizes and honors. They symbolize the approval and appreciation of others, whether it's an Employee of the Month trophy, a plaque for sales achievement, or the sign declaring yours as the neighborhood's prettiest yard.

Such prizes and awards are often the culmination of the pursuit of personal achievement and accomplishment. They represent accolades and recognition from the world. Nothing is inherently wrong with any of that as long as we keep them in perspective.

That is, we must never let such awards become idols that we worship or lower our sight from the greatest prize of all and the only one truly worth winning. It's one that won't rust, collect dust, or leave us wondering why we worked so hard to win it in the first place. The ultimate prize is eternal life, and it's ours through Jesus Christ.

You can take all the victory trophies and stuff them in a corner. I want the trophy that comes with the championship.
-- Jimmie Johnson crew chief Chad Knaus

The greatest prize of all doesn't require competition to claim it; God has it ready to hand to you through Jesus Christ.

LIVE ACTION

Read James 2:14-26.

"Faith by itself, if it is not accompanied by action, is dead"
(v. 17).

Words started it all, but it took ten months of action to make those words prophetic.

The start of the 2007 NASCAR season was still twenty-six days away on Tuesday, Jan. 23, when team owner Rick Hendrick showed up at the Hendrick Motorsports headquarters in Charlotte. He shook hands with a few of his drivers and crew chiefs and then made his way through the crowd to mount a podium.

Hendrick had something to say to the 550 folks who made up his race team: "If we keep working at it, we can win the championship again this year. Nobody has the talent and depth that we have in this room. Let's just stay focused on what's important, and that's bringing home another trophy."

Sports Illustrated's Lars Anderson noted the speech "may not have been the stuff of Rockne or Lombardi, but the crowd thundered in applause. Hendrick's words clearly lit a fire inside of everyone in his organization."

The proof was in the results. Ten months later, the Hendrick team and their owner reigned over NASCAR as no other had since the beginning of the Chase format. His drivers won 18 of the 36 races with Jimmie Johnson the Cup champion for the second straight year, Jeff Gordon second, and Kyle Busch fifth.

"This is about as good of a year as an owner could ever hope to have," Hendrick said before the final race of the year. "It's just been a dream kind of season."

The dream season ended in the warmth of south Florida, but it had begun in the chill of North Carolina with a speech. The words were effective in generating some momentary enthusiasm among the team members, but of themselves they didn't accomplish very much. They had to be followed by action for goals to be achieved and victories to be earned.

Talk is cheap. Consider your neighbor or coworker who talks without saying anything, who makes promises she doesn't keep, who brags about his own exploits, who can always tell you how to do something but never shows up for the work.

How often have you fidgeted through a meeting, impatient to get on with the work everybody is talking about doing? You know – just as Rick Hendrick did when he told his team to keep working and stay focused -- that speech without action just doesn't cut it.

That principle applies in the life of a person of faith too. Merely declaring our faith isn't enough, however sincere we may be. It is putting our faith into action that shouts to the world of the depth of our commitment to Christ. Just as Jesus' ministry was a virtual whirlwind of activity, so are we to change the world by doing.

Jesus Christ is alive; so should our faith in Him be.

You can talk about it all day, but you can't put into words the feelings you have inside.
                    -- Dale Earnhardt after winning the 1998 Daytona 500

Faith that does not reveal itself in action is dead.

DAY 26

AS A RULE

Read Luke 5:27-32.

"Why do you eat and drink with tax collectors and 'sinners'?" (v. 30b)

A widespread perception exists that NASCAR's rules are somewhat flexible, to put it kindly.

Writer Monte Dutton once characterized stock-car racing's governing body as "famously arbitrary," playing "fast and loose" with the rules. This impression is not limited to the NASCAR fraternity. A college basketball coach once asked about the rules at a celebrity golf tournament hosted by a driver and then cracked, "Oh, I forgot, this is NASCAR. There aren't any rules, are there?" Then-Vice President Dick Cheney famously observed that what went on in the ruling body's command center "is sometimes more exciting than what happens in the race itself."

Dutton wrote that "NASCAR's administration of Cup races sometimes [is] marked by judgment calls that are subjective and capricious, . . . the rules seemingly influenced by timing, the relative prominence of the competitors involved and the effect on the outcome." The perception of NASCAR's capriciousness extends even to the use of the notorious "debris caution" -- throwing a caution flag late in the race because of debris that may or may not be present -- to keep races close that are threatening to get out of hand or to give prominent drivers a break.

Dutton noted that this "management style is as old as the ruling body itself," so no matter how frustrating it often is to drivers and fans alike, it's not going away. "This sport has a tremendous amount of things that aren't in writing," driver Jeff Burton once said. "The harder that you run and the more aggressive you are, your code is going to be different than another guy."

You live by rules others set up. Some lender determined the interest rate on your mortgage and your car loan. You work hours and shifts somebody else established. Someone else decided what day your garbage gets picked up and what school district your house is in.

Jesus encountered societal rules also, including a strict set of religious edicts that dictated what company he should keep, what people, in other words, were fit for him to socialize with, talk to, or share a meal with. Jesus ignored the rules, choosing love instead of mindless obedience and demonstrating his disdain for society's rules by mingling with the outcasts, the lowlifes, the poor, and the misfits.

You, too, have to choose when you find yourself in the presence of someone whom society deems undesirable. Will you choose the rules or love? Are you willing to be a rebel for love — as Jesus was for you?

It's a matter of what mood officials are in when they're sitting in the booth that night, to be honest with you.
                                        -- Kevin Harvick on NASCAR's rules

**Society's rules dictate who is acceptable
and who is not, but love in the name of Jesus
knows no such distinctions.**

FOUND WANTING

Read Psalm 73:23-28.

*"Whom have I in heaven but you? And earth has nothing
I desire besides you" (v. 25).*

Tom Higgins once wrote, "Deep within, every race driver harbors a wish to have a car so fast that it appears to be a blur." Buddy
Baker got one.

In the 1980 Daytona 500, Baker drove an Oldsmobile so quick
"that NASCAR officials ordered pink Day-Glo strips taped to the
car's front end to enable rivals being overtaken by Big Buddy to
see him coming."

Intent on getting Baker his first Daytona 500 victory after two
decades of trying, Baker's team owner, Harry Ranier, told crew
chief and engine builder Waddell Wilson "to do whatever it took
within reason and within the rules to give Buddy a car he could
put in Victory Lane."

Wilson farmed out the work to a friend's shop. When the
company finished building the car that would be dubbed the Gray
Ghost, they brought it and the bill to Wilson. "It was $10,000! I
almost fainted," Wilson recalled. "That was about five times what
we were paying for a body in those days. I said to myself, 'Harry
is going to fire me, and then he's going to kill me.'"

After Baker won the pole, some team owners tried to convince
Bill France, Jr. that the Ghost was illegal. So inspectors gave the
car a second going over. "They didn't find one thing illegal about

it," Wilson said. "We had pushed the envelope to the limit, I admit, but everything about that car was within the rules."

Baker and the Ghost won Daytona with the fastest average speed of any type car in a 500-mile race. When presented the bill, Ranier smiled, shrugged, and didn't say a word. Everyone had what he wanted.

What do you want out of life? A loving, caring family, a home of your own, the respect of those whom you admire? Our heart's desires can elevate us to greatness and goodness, but they can also plunge us into destruction, despair, and evil. Drugs, alcohol, control, sex, power, worldly success: Do these desires motivate you?

Desires are not inherently evil or bad for you; after all, God planted the capacity to desire in us. The key is determining which of your heart's desires are healthful and are worth pursuing and which are dangerous and are best avoided.

Not surprisingly, the answer to the dilemma lies with God. You consult the one whose own heart's desire is for what is unequivocally best for you, who is driven only by his unqualified love for you. You match what you want for yourself with what God wants for you. Your deepest heart's desire must be the establishment and maintenance of an intimate relationship with God.

Ya gotta wanna.

-- *Dick Trickle*

**Whether our desires drive us to greatness
or to destruction is determined by whether
they are also God's desires for our lives.**

BE PREPARED

Read Matthew 10:5-23.

"I am sending you out like sheep among wolves. Therefore be as shrewd as snakes and as innocent as doves" (v. 16).

In a NASCAR race, inches measured by seconds lost or gained really matter, and they often depend upon the readiness of a pit crew.

Lee Petty recalled that in his day pit stops sometimes lasted as long as three minutes and "races were won on the track solely with brawn and guts." A dramatic change came with the Wood Brothers racing team in the early 1960s when their pit crews began practicing for the stops and then hustling all the way through them. The team called them "speed stops," and they helped them win that day. Others quickly saw what a difference the shortened pit stops made, and they followed suit until the pit stop evolved into what is truly one of the most synchronized and beautiful routines in all of sport.

As you would expect, such excellence requires extensive preparation. Today's pit crews often train five days a week, repeating every step until they have mastered the routine. They work with professional trainers to improve their strength, even mimicking a real pit stop while carrying 45-pound medicine balls. They also video-tape and analyze their practices to spot flaws. A tire carrier who was a former college football player once observed that the pit-crew practices were as tough as any football practice he had ever experienced. Today's crews are in effect "well-trained athletes masked as pit crew members."

When race-day comes, the pit crew is prepared to save those precious seconds that become inches that often determine the winner.

You know the importance of preparation in your own life. You went to the bank for a car loan, facts and figures in hand. That presentation you made at work was seamless because you practiced. The kids' school play suffered no meltdowns because they rehearsed. Knowing what you need to do and doing what you must to succeed isn't luck; it's preparation.

Jesus understood this, and he prepared his followers by lecturing them and by sending them on field trips. Two thousand years later, the life of faith requires similar training and study. You prepare so you'll be ready when that unsaved neighbor standing beside you at your backyard grill asks about Jesus. You prepare so you will know how God wants you to live. You prepare so you are certain in what you believe when the secular, godless world challenges it.

And one day you'll see God face to face. You certainly want to be prepared for that.

Making better pit stops comes from harder work back at the shop, practicing, testing, trying to get better.

-- Dale Earnhardt

Living in faith requires constant study and training, preparation for the day when you meet God face to face.

RIGHT ON

Read Galatians 6:7-10.

"Let us not grow weary in doing what is right, for we will reap at harvest time, if we do not give up" (v. 9 NRSV).

Legendary country singer Marty Robbins was an avid racing fan, and, as he proved one day after a race, an honorable man who did the right thing.

In *"Then Junior Said to Jeff . . .,"* David Poole and Jim McLaurin declared that Robbins "loved racing as much as he did singing." He often left the Grand Ole Opry as soon as he finished performing so he could race with the locals in Nashville. But singing was his livelihood while racing was a hobby. He never had enough money to be a challenger, but he "enjoyed racing back in the pack with the rest of the 'independents.'"

In 1972 at Talledega Superspeedway, however, Robbins did much more than run back with the independents. He ran faster than he expected and found himself among the leaders. He was clocked at 188 mph while he had qualified at only 177 mph, and he finished 18th.

Rather than congratulating himself, though, Robbins figured something was wrong. He asked a NASCAR technical inspector to check out his carburetor. Sure enough, unbeknownst to Robbins, someone had installed one that was larger than it should have been. Robbins refused the $250 bonus for being the highest-finishing rookie, and NASCAR disqualified him for the illegal carburetor.

Robbins lost more than $1,000, but more important than the money was his honor. He did the right thing. He also said it was worth it just to see the look on some drivers' faces when he blew by them.

Doing the right thing is easy when it's little stuff. Giving the quarter back when the cashier gives you too much change, helping a lost child at the mall, or putting a few bucks in the honor box at your favorite fishing hole.

But what about when it costs you? Every day you have multiple chances to do the right thing; in every instance, you have a choice: right or wrong. The factors that weigh into your decisions – including the personal cost to you – reveal much about your character.

But what if there's a chance you could get away with not doing the right thing and thus can avoid the personal cost? Does your doing the right thing ever depend upon your calculation of the odds of getting caught? In the world's eyes, you can't go wrong doing wrong when you won't get caught. That certainly passes for the world's slippery, situational ethics, but it doesn't pass muster with God.

In God's eyes, you can't go wrong doing right. Ever.

We've got to conduct ourselves properly if we're going to play on the big stage. We've got to conduct ourselves with integrity.
-- Texas Motor Speedway President Eddie Gossage

**As far as God is concerned,
you can never go wrong doing right.**

DECIDE FOR YOURSELF

Read John 6:60-69.

"The words I have spoken to you are spirit and they are life. Yet there are some of you who do not believe" (vv. 63b-64a).

In 1955 Clay Earles made a decision that irrevocably changed NASCAR.

Earles was one of the men instrumental in the founding of NASCAR. He loved racing so much that he built the Martins-ville Speedway from scratch, not to make any money, but just to see races. He actually built the track before NASCAR existed. "I told myself it would be a nice hobby," Earles said. He originally intended to run Indy cars on his track, but soon after he finished his track, Bill France began the sanctioning body called NASCAR and Earles changed his mind.

His first race was on Sept. 7, 1947, and France came and parked cars for him, helping Earles get his track off the ground. In return, Earles helped France run NASCAR. In 1949, NASCAR's first year, the sixth race was held at Martinsville.

Earles had 6,013 people at that first race -- but there was a real problem. "Ladies had come here that day from church with their Sunday best on," Earles recalled, and they and everybody else got covered with dust. After that first race, attendance averaged only around 3,000 fans, and it stayed down until 1955. That's when Earles decided to do something nobody else had ever done: pave his track.

In all sincerity, France asked if paving the truck would ruin racing. Earles answered, "I'll tell you this, Bill. If I don't pave it, I'm ruined." So he paved it and the first race after that drew more than twelve thousand people. Earles had discovered something, and NASCAR was never the same again.

As it was with Clay Earles, the decisions you have made along the way have shaped your life at every pivotal moment. Some decisions you made suddenly and carelessly; some you made carefully and deliberately; some were forced upon you. Some of those spur-of-the-moment decisions probably have turned out better than your carefully considered ones.

Of all your life's decisions, however, none is more important than one you cannot ignore: What have you done with Jesus? Even in his time, people chose to follow Jesus or to reject him, and nothing has changed; the decision must still be made and nobody can make it for you. Ignoring Jesus won't work either; that is, in fact, a decision, and neither he nor the consequences of your decision will go away.

Carefully considered or spontaneous – how you arrive at a decision for Jesus doesn't matter; all that matters is that you get there.

I always put a lot of thought into everything I do. A lot of us don't do enough thinking.

-- *Clay Earles*

A decision for Jesus may be spontaneous or considered; what counts is that you make it.

TRICK PLAY

Read Acts 19:11-20.

"The evil spirit answered them, 'Jesus I know, and I know about Paul, but who are you?'" (v. 15)

At Watkins Glen in 1994, crew chief Larry McReynolds and his crew tried to steal a victory for Ernie Irvan with a trick play.

After the tragic death of Davey Allison in a helicopter crash in 1993, team owner Robert Yates and McReynolds were left with the virtually impossible task of finding an equally talented driver. Some critical timing helped them out as they eventually closed a deal with Irvan, who was "fussing and fighting, mostly over money" with his team owners.

As McReynolds recalled it, Irvan and Mark Martin dueled all day long at Wakins Glen. Martin had the lead late with Irvan running second. "Track position is important at Watkins Glen," McReynolds said, "because restarts are single file." So with about ten laps to go, McReynolds and his team decided they'd try to trick Martin and let Irvan grab the lead even though everyone knew both teams had tires and fuel to make it to the end.

They had no intention of pitting, but the crew "got up on the pit wall and [McReynolds] held up four fingers, we held out the sign, we got all our guys in position." They were trying to trick Martin into thinking that Irvan was pitting so he would pit and then Irvan would stay on the track and take the lead.

It almost worked. "All of a sudden I could see that 6 team

scrambling," McReynolds said. "They didn't know what to do" because they could see Irvan's crew "all geared up" for a pit stop. "If we pitted, they figured they'd have to pit," McReynolds said.

At the last moment, though, Martin figured out what was going on and stayed on the track, as did Irvan. Martin won the race, and Irvan finished second.

The trick play didn't work that time.

Scam artists are everywhere — and they love trick plays. An e-mail encourages you to send money to some foreign country to get rich. That guy at your front door offers to resurface your driveway at a ridiculously low price. A TV ad promises a pill to help you lose weight without diet or exercise.

You've been around; you check things out before deciding. The same approach is necessary with spiritual matters, too, because false religions and bogus Christian denominations abound. The key is what any group does with Jesus. Is he the son of God, the ruler of the universe, and the only way to salvation? If not, then what the group espouses is something other than the true Word of God.

The good news about Jesus does indeed sound too good to be true. But the only catch is that there is no catch. No trick -- just the truth.

I have a trick. I look into the camera lens and I can see them reflecting on my shirt.
      -- Carl Edwards on how he could remember all his sponsors

God's promises through Jesus sound too good to be true, but the only catch is that there is no catch.

FATHERS AND SONS

Read Matthew 3:13-17.

"A voice from heaven said, 'This is my Son, whom I love; with him I am well pleased'" (v. 17).

Buddy Baker had a tough, demanding teacher; that same teacher was also the first driver to ever bump him in a race. The teacher was his dad, Buck Baker.

Buck Baker was the racing champion in 1956 and '57; in 1959, Buddy followed in his successful dad's tire tracks. "I was brought up not only in a racing family but in a winning environment," Buddy recalled. "When I was a boy, my heroes were all in racing."

He called it "pretty spooky" when he made the decision to race. Said Buddy, "If you've ever spoken to my dad, he can be pretty hard-line when it comes to things -- they have to make a lot of sense." He nevertheless wanted his father's blessing.

He was working in his dad's race shop, and he approached Buck twice before he worked up the courage to tell him. Buck's response "almost floored" his son. He said, "See that old car in the corner over there? Get you some people and put it together and you can run this weekend." Buddy got the car put together and entered his first race.

And his dad took it easy on him, right? Uh -- no. Buddy recalled, "I got a little bit wide, and [my father] rapped me, and I was knocked almost into the infield. My own dad! So the first

NASCAR

car that ever put a fender on me was my own father!" One lesson -- among many -- Buddy learned from his dad.

Buddy never really thought about proving himself to his dad by outrunning him, though he eventually did just that. "I always respected my father. I never went, 'I beat my father.' I never had any joy of finishing ahead of him."

American society largely belittles and marginalizes fathers and their influence upon their sons. Men are perceived as necessary to effect pregnancy; after that, they can leave and everybody's better off.

But we need look in only two places to appreciate the enormity of that misconception: our jails – packed with males who lacked the influence of fathers in their lives as they grew up -- and the Bible. God – being God – could have chosen any relationship he desired between Jesus and himself, including society's approach of irrelevancy. Instead, the most important relationship in all of history was that of father-son. God obviously believes a close, loving relationship between fathers and sons, such as that of Buck and Buddy Baker, is crucial. For men and women to espouse otherwise or for men to walk blithely and carelessly out of their children's lives constitutes disobedience to the divine will.

Simply put, God loves fathers. After all, he is one.

My father was my all-time special person.

-- Buddy Baker

Fatherhood is a tough job, but a model for the father-child relationship is found in that of Jesus the Son with God the Father.

DAY 33

WORM DROWNING

Read Mark 1:16-20.

*"'Come, follow me,' Jesus said, 'and I will make you
fishers of men'" (v. 17).*

If the story Benny Parsons told about a fishing trip is true (You know how suspect those fishing tales are!), "Handsome" Harry Gant is NASCAR's greatest fisherman ever.

Gant won eighteen races and finished in the top ten 208 times during a 22-year career that ended with his retirement after the 1994 season. He received his nickname because of his Hollywood-style good lucks; he even appeared in the Burt Reynolds movie *Stoker Ace*. When he won at Martinsville in 1982, he was the oldest driver ever to drive to his first career Cup victory.

In 1984, U.S. Tobacco Co. rewarded its drivers with a fishing trip to Alaska. Polite to a fault, none of the "fishermen" told their host that they didn't fish.

Parsons said that on the third day of the trip Gant waded out to the middle of the Wood River and started catching one rainbow trout after another "that look about as long as your arm," releasing each fish after he caught it. No matter what he did, Gant caught fish as soon as he cast, counting them to rub it in. He caught eighteen fish in eighteen casts and suddenly quit. "There ain't nothing to this," he grinned. "I'm gonna take me a nap."

As he waded to the shore with his rod over his shoulder, Gant accidentally pushed the button that dropped his lure into the water. The other fishermen watched incredulously as another trout grabbed Gant's spinner. "Nineteen in a row!" Gant shouted. Parsons said that as Gant came by him he winked and said, "I've got to get out of this river. They're chasing me!"

The worst fishing trip you ever had may have included numbing cold, nary a nibble, a flat tire, or any combination of misadventures. You dragged in late, knowing full well you had to get up early next morning. Still, it was better than a good day at work, wasn't it?

What if somebody in authority looked you square in the eyes and told you, "Go Fish"? How quickly would you trip over anybody who got in your way? Well, Jesus did exactly that, commanding his followers to fish for people who are drowning and lost without him.

Jesus issued that command with the utmost seriousness. For the men of his time, fishing was neither for pleasure nor for sport. Rather, it was hard work, a demanding, hardscrabble way to support a family.

Fishing for men and women for Jesus is likewise hard work, but it is such the essence of the Christian mission that a fish has become the symbol of the faith itself.

I can't go fishing in my own lake because of Neil. Because we fished in it all the time. I can't. I've tried. It's Neil's pond.
        -- Dale Earnhardt after the death of Neil Bonnett

Jesus understood the passion people have for fishing and commanded that it become not just a hobby but a way of life.

REGRETS, ANYONE?

Read 2 Corinthians 7:8-13.

"Godly sorrow brings repentance that leads to salvation and leaves no regret" (v. 10).

Fred Lorenzen made a decision he regretted.

In his prime, Lorenzen was one of NASCAR's greatest ever. Nicknamed "The Golden Boy," he won twenty-six races from 1961 through 1967, including the 1965 Daytona 500. In 1998, he was named one of NASCAR's 50 Greatest Drivers, and he was inducted in 2001 into the Motorsports Hall of Fame of America.

By 1967, though, he had apparently lost his enthusiasm for racing. He started only five races that year with one win and one second-place finish. As Joe Menzer put it, Lorenzen then "surprised the racing community by saying he was retiring -- a decision he would later regret."

His regret showed itself in his decision in 1970 to try racing again. He started seven races that year, but finished in the top ten only once. In 1971, he started fourteen races and finished higher than fourth only once. "The whispers had begun that he just couldn't win like he used to" because his skills had diminished during his time off.

Lorenzen disagreed, convinced he could win again. He returned in 1972, making eight starts, but never came close to winning another race. After that season, he retired for good.

In his later years, Lorenzen drove a Junior-Johnson-owned

NASCAR

Ford that drivers called "The Yellow Banana" because of its aerodynamic design. When Lorenzen crashed it at the Dixie 500, one pit crew member said he wasn't surprised by the wreck: "I ain't never seen anybody who could drive a banana at 150 miles an hour."

His career interrupted by his premature retirement, Lorenzen just could never regain the golden touch.

In their hit "The Class of '57," the Statler Brothers served up some pure country truth when they sang, "Things get complicated when you get past 18." That complication includes regrets; you have them; so does everyone else: situations and relationships that upon reflection we wish we had handled differently.

Feeling troubled or remorseful over something you've done or left undone is not necessarily a bad thing. That's because God uses regrets to spur us to repentance, which is the decision to change our ways. Repentance in turn is essential to salvation through Jesus Christ. You regret your un-Christlike actions, repent by promising God to mend your ways, and then seek and receive forgiveness for them.

The cold, hard truth is that you will have more regrets in your life. You can know absolutely, however, that you will never ever regret making Jesus the reason for that life.

Looking back now, I would've done things differently when I was young and dumb.

-- Jeremy Mayfield

Regrets are part of living, but you'll never regret living for Jesus.

PRECIOUS MEMORIES

Read 1 Thessalonians 3:6-13.

"Timothy . . . has brought good news about your faith and love. He has told us that you always have pleasant memories of us" (v. 6).

Writer Tom Higgins remembered vividly the last time he saw Davey Allison alive.

The son of Bobby Allison, Davey, who won nineteen races in his truncated career, was 32 when he was killed on July 11, 1993, in the crash landing of his helicopter at Talladega Superspeedway.

Higgins had waited with Allison at New Hampshire International Speedway for the helicopter that would ferry Allison to a nearby airport and the plane ride home. Higgins wrote, "I, along with many others, watched as the helicopter flew into a setting New England sun." Allison made that trip home successfully, but less than 48 hours later, he was dead.

Higgins also remembered where he was when he heard the awful news: Higgins Beach, Maine, near Portland. He remembered Allison's competitive nature, inherited from his father, who won 85 races and the 1983 Cup championship. He remembered that Allison and he shared a passion for fishing, that he didn't get to fulfill a promise he had made to Allison that at Higgins Beach he would catch a striper for him. The helicopter crash ended the fishing trip.

Months later, Higgins did catch that striper on North Carolina's

Outer Banks. He "stroked it gently, took the hook from its mouth, and slid it back into the sea in memory of Davey Allison."

Tom Higgins remembered.

Your whole life, too, will one day be only a memory because – hold your breath for this red-hot news flash -- you will die. With that knowledge in hand, you can get busy and make some preparations for that fateful day by selecting a funeral home, purchasing a cemetery plot and picking out your casket or opting for cremation and choosing a tasteful urn, designating those who will deliver your eulogy, and even making other less important decisions about your send-off.

What you cannot control about your death, however, is how you will be remembered and whether your demise leaves a gaping hole in the lives of those with whom you shared your life or a pothole that's quickly paved over. What determines whether those nice words someone will say about you are heartfelt truth or pleasant fabrications? What determines whether the tears that fall at your death result from heartfelt grief or a sinus infection?

Love does. Just as Paul wrote, the love you give away during your life decides whether or not memories of you will be precious and pleasant.

I want people to remember Davey [Allison] as a God-driven person with family number one in his heart and doing something he loved.
--Liz Allison

How you will be remembered after you die
is largely determined by how much
and how deeply you love others now.

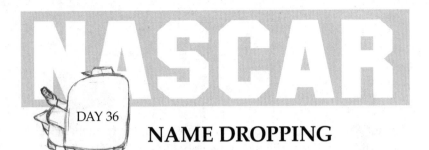

DAY 36

NAME DROPPING

Read Exodus 3:13-20.

*"God said to Moses, 'I AM WHO I AM. This is what
you are to say to the Israelites: 'I AM has sent me to you'"
(v. 14).*

Is not "Fireball" Roberts the greatest nickname ever slapped
upon a NASCAR racer? A close second, though, must surely be
Awesome Bill from Dawsonville.

Throughout the years, the men involved in the world's
greatest sport have often wound up with colorful and descriptive
nicknames. Richard Petty will always be The King, and Dale
Earnhardt will live forever as The Intimidator.

"Tiny" Lund actually stood six feet five, weighed more than 250
pounds, and was once described as "built like a tank." Legendary
car builder Edwin Keith Matthews will forever be known as
"Banjo," a nickname hung on him in grade school because of his
thick glasses.

"Handsome" Harry Gant. Henry "Smokey" Yunick, so named
because of the way a motorcycle he built smoked up the track.
Herman "the Turtle" Beam, whose strategy was to build a good
car, stay out of everybody's way for three or four hours, and
collect his winnings.

H.A. "Humpy" Wheeler acquired his unusual nickname
from his college football teammates after his coach caught him
smoking Camel cigarettes and made him run laps as punishment.

"Suitcase" Jake Elder was nicknamed because of his tendency to change teams. Danny "Chocolate" Myers. Charles "Slick" Owens. David Pearson aka "The Silver Fox." Remember "Chargin' Charlie" Glotzbach, nicknamed for his driving style? And what name *was* Junior Johnson, The Ronda Roadrunner, given at his birth? Nicknames such as Tony Stewart's "Smoke" are not slapped haphazardly upon individuals but rather reflect widely held perceptions about the person named. Proper names do that also.

Nowhere throughout history has this concept been more prevalent that in the Bible, where a name is not a mere label but is an expression of the essential nature of the named one. That is, a person's name reveals his or her character. Even God shares this concept; to know the name of God is to know God as he has chosen to reveal himself to us.

What does your name say about you? Honest, trustworthy, a seeker of the truth and a person of God? Or does the mention of your name cause your coworkers to whisper snide remarks, your neighbors to roll their eyes, or your friends to start making allowances for you?

Most importantly, what does your name say about you to God? He, too, knows you by name.

The idea that someone was called "Fireball" was just repugnant to me.
-- Judy Judge on Glenn Roberts, the love of her life

Live so that your name evokes
positive associations by people you know,
by the public, and by God.

DUMB MOVE

Read 1 Kings 4:29-34; 11:1-6.

"As Solomon grew old, his wives turned his heart after other gods, and his heart was not fully devoted to the Lord his God" (v. 4).

The lore generated by Daytona's legendary water and beach course includes the story Tom Higgins relates of a Connecticut Yankee who decided on an impulse to enter the race.

From 1936-41 and from 1946-58, stock car races were run on a 4.1-mile beach layout that consisted of about two miles of hard-packed sand, two miles of Highway US-A1A, and two hairpin turns.

That Connecticut Yankee had driven down in his brand new Nash to watch one of those legendary beach races when he indulged his whim. NASCAR rules being what they were back in those days, he was allowed to enter the field. He promptly got involved in a multi-car wreck and totaled his nice new car.

He rode a bus back to Connecticut and a cab to his house where he was met by his wife, who, not surprisingly, noticed he didn't have the car with him. The cornered hubby promptly broke into sobs. "Baby, I'm lucky to be alive," he managed. "I was caught in one of them horrible Florida hurricanes and the car was swept out to sea. I can't believe I got out of it and made it home to you!" Totally ignorant of the fact that Florida's hurricane season was months away, the wife bought his story.

The quick thinker once told Higgins that he got lucky twice. "The wreck should have killed me. And if she'd ever found out the truth, what she would have inflicted on me would have been worse than any injury in a car wreck."

As far as is known, he never repeated his astonishingly dumb move again.

Remember that time you wrecked the car when you spilled hot coffee on your lap? That cold morning you fell out of the boat? The time you gave your honey a tool box for her birthday?

Formal education notwithstanding, we all make some dumb moves sometime because time spent in a classroom is not an accurate gauge of common sense. Folks impressed with their own smarts often grace us with erudite pronouncements that we intuitively recognize as flawed, unworkable, or simply wrong.

A good example is the observation that great intelligence and scholarship are not compatible with faith in God. That is, the more we know, the less we believe. But any incompatibility occurs only because we begin to trust in our own wisdom rather than the wisdom of God. We forget, as Solomon did, that God is the ultimate source of all our knowledge and wisdom and that even our ability to learn is a gift from God.

Not smart at all.

Judging by some of the stupid things I do, I feel like I'm 18.
                                        -- Jimmie Johnson in 2007

**Being truly smart means trusting in God
rather than only in your own smarts.**

IN THE KNOW

Read John 4:19-26, 39-42.

"They said to the woman, . . . 'Now we have heard for ourselves, and we know that this man really is the Savior of the world'" (v. 42).

After a lifetime of experience with stock car racing, Danny "Chocolate" Myers observed, "A hundred years from now they're going to look back and say [that Dale Earnhardt is] the greatest driver that's ever been." It wasn't just Earnhardt's skills behind the wheel that made him the best, Myers said. It was also that Earnhardt knew things other mortals didn't.

Myers was a mechanic and the gas man for the #3 GM Goodwrench Chevy Earnhardt drove. He was one of the most popular and most recognizable crew members in the world with his great bulk and bushy black beard. When NASCAR raced in Japan in 1996, he was mobbed for autographs.

He knew, therefore, of what he spoke when he said Earnhardt knew things other folks didn't. Once when the Richard Childress racing team was testing at Bristol, Earnhardt ran a few laps and came in. "The crankshaft is broken," he said. "I felt it." The crew was dumbfounded. "You felt the crankshaft break?" Myers asked, believing that such a thing was impossible. When they raised the hood up, everything looked all right. Someone said crank it up, but Earnhardt insisted. "Don't do that," he said. "I'm pretty sure the crankshaft is broken."

NASCAR

So the crew took a screwdriver, stuck it down the front of the engine, and discovered -- the crankshaft was broken. Myers asked Earnhardt how he knew. "My dad would sometimes make me drive barefoot so I could feel it," he explained.

Once at Talladega running at 200 miles an hour, Earnhardt passed a car and told his crew, "They're about to blow a piston. I smelled it when I went by." Sure enough, a couple of laps later the car blew up and was gone.

Dale Earnhardt just knew.

He just knew in the same way you know certain things in your life. That your spouse loves you, for instance. That you are good at your job. That tea should be iced and sweetened. That friendship is lifelong. That the best barbecue comes from a pig. You know these things even though no mathematician or philosopher can prove any of this on paper.

It's the same way with faith in Jesus: You just know that he is God's son and the savior of the world. You know it in the same way that you know your favorite driver is the only one worth pulling for: with every fiber of your being, with all your heart, your mind, and your soul.

You just know, and because you know him, Jesus knows you. And that is all you really need to know.

I would like to thank everybody. You know who you are and your last names.

-- *Ward Burton after a victory*

A life of faith is lived in certainty and conviction:
You just know you know.

SEEING THE VISION

Read Acts 26:1, 9-23.

"So then, . . . I was not disobedient to the vision from heaven" (v. 19).

They were father-and-son visionaries who created NASCAR and morphed it into the worldwide sport it is today.

Bill France, Sr. was the great builder of NASCAR. He was the one who came up with the "far-reaching, far-thinking brilliant idea that the cars that ran in all NASCAR events would be late model cars." France Sr. was the one who believed that "race fans would be most interested in watching race cars that looked like the ones they were buying in showrooms across America."

Writer Max Muhleman described France Sr. as a "master politician with a great sense of timing," and a "benevolent dictator," who "on balance . . . was a genius." When deposed dictator Fulgencio Batista fled Cuba in 1959 for the friendlier environs of Daytona Beach, Muhleman drew France's wrath by declaring in a column, "Now there are two dictators in Daytona Beach, Fulgencio Batista and Bill France."

While NASCAR would not exist at all without the senior France, his son, Bill France, Jr., wrote Steve McCormick, "had the vision and drive to make NASCAR what it is today." He "did whatever needed to be done. He was a flagman, official, scorer, promoter and more in his NASCAR career."

The modern era of NASCAR actually began in 1972 when

senior handed control of the sport to his son, an event described in the International Motorsports Hall of Fame as "the most significant event in the history of the sanctioning body" other than the founding of NASCAR itself. Writer Mark Aumann said, France Jr. took his father's original vision and transformed it "into something greater than the sum of its parts." He led the evolution of NASCAR from a regional sport to a worldwide phenomenon.

To speak of visions is often to risk their being lumped with palm readings, Ouija boards, seances, horoscopes, and other such useless mumbo-jumbo. The danger such mild amusements pose, however, is very real in that they indicate a reliance on something other than God. It is God who knows the future; it is God who has a vision and a plan for your life; it is God who has the answers you seek as you struggle to find your way.

You probably do have a vision for your life, a plan for how it should unfold. It's the dream you pursue through your family, your job, your hobbies, your interests. But your vision inspires a fruitful life only if it is compatible with God's plan. As the apostle Paul found out, you ignore God's vision at your peril. But if you pursue it, you'll find an even more glorious life than you could ever have envisioned for yourself.

Bill France, Sr. was the architect of NASCAR, but Bill France, Jr. proved to be the ultimate general manager.

-- Writer Mark Auhmann

Your grandest vision for the future will pale beside the vision God has of what the two of you can accomplish together.

THE SCAPEGOAT

Read Leviticus 16:15-22.

"He is to lay both hands on the head of the live goat and confess over it all the wickedness and rebellion of the Israelites — all their sins — and put them on the goat's head" (v. 21).

Looking for ways to make his work easier, a young Dale Jarrett once came up with the brilliant idea of having some goats help him out. They did a good job all right; they did too good a job.

A two-time Grand National champion, Ned Jarrett was named one of NASCAR's 50 Greatest Drivers in 1998. He won fifty times in a 13-year career. In 1965, he set a record that will probably never be broken by winning the Southern 500 at Darlington by fourteen laps, a distance of 19 and one-quarter miles.

Ned Jarrett went out on top, retiring in 1966 when he was only 34. He is the only driver to retire as the NASCAR champion. He went back home to run the Hickory Motor Speedway, the track where he had first raced. He hired among others his 20-year-old son, Dale, a star athlete in high school who had been offered a golf scholarship to the University of South Carolina but had decided he didn't want to go to college.

The younger Jarrett was charged with doing everything from selling popcorn to driving the pace car to mowing the grass. Not enjoying that grass cutting very much, Dale came up with the inspired notion of bringing in some goats to do the job.

NASCAR

As Dale would say years later, it seemed like a good idea at the time. Oh, the goats ate the grass all right. They also chowed down on the seats and the dashboards of the old cars Ned kept for use in demolition derbies.

Under orders from his chagrined boss, Dale quickly retired the goats.

A particular type of goat -- a scapegoat – could really be useful. Mess up at work? Bring him in to get chewed out. Make a decision your children don't like? Let him put up with the whining and complaining. Forget your anniversary? Call him in to grovel and explain.

What a set-up! You don't have to pay the price for your mistakes, your shortcomings, and your failures. You get off scot-free. Exactly the way forgiveness works with Jesus.

Our sins separate us from God because we the unholy can't stand in the presence of the holy God. To remove our guilt, God requires a blood sacrifice. Out of his unimaginable love for us, he provided the sacrifice: his own son. Jesus is the sacrifice made for us; through Jesus and Jesus alone, forgiveness and eternity with God are ours.

It's a bumper sticker, but it's true: We aren't perfect; we're just forgiven.

Before a driver starts asking the crew to make changes on the car, he has to figure out how much of the problem is him.

-- *Rocky Moran*

**For all those times you fail God, you have Jesus
to take the guilt and the blame for you.**

THE SNAKE PIT

Read Matthew 23:29-39.

"You snakes! You brood of vipers! How will you escape being condemned to hell?" (v. 33)

For a few terrifying moments, Tiny Lund once shared his ride with a live rattlesnake -- courtesy of Cale Yarborough.

Yarborough and Lund were close friends and practical jokers. Yarborough once dumped a bucket of ice water on Lund while he was in the shower. A livid Lund chased Yarborough until he realized he was standing naked in the parking lot -- in front of an elderly lady. He tipped an imaginary cap, muttered "Pardon me, Ma'am," and tiptoed away.

Once on race day, Lund tossed a rubber snake into Yarborough's car after he had climbed in. Yarborough's panic and fear were real and extreme until he realized the snake was fake.

A week later an inspired Yarborough returned the favor in spades. An accomplished handler of rattlesnakes, Yarborough caught a live one and pulled its fangs out. He then waited until his big buddy had strapped himself in and tossed the extremely angry snake onto Lund's lap. Lund instantly realized this snake wasn't fake -- and it was alive.

While Lund "screamed bloody murder" and the snake rattled its tail, Yarborough and a few friends he had tipped off howled with glee. Since Lund was a giant of a man, strapping him into his car was no small deal. Getting out in panic wasn't easy either, though Lund escaped from "that car considerably faster than he went in." He then chased Yarborough with a ball peen hammer until a couple of men restrained him to prevent any permanent damage to Yarborough's head.

Who would want to be known as a snake-in-the-grass? Or to be so unlucky, you're snake bit? Don't roll snake eyes if you're foolish enough to gamble, and don't drink any snake oil for medicinal help.

Snakes and mankind have never exactly been bosom buddies. The Old Testament often uses snakes (and serpents) as metaphors for something or someone who is dangerous and wicked. Thus, Jesus had a great scriptural tradition undergirding his referring to religious leaders as snakes.

Jesus' point was that the religious folks were wicked and dangerous because they appeared faithful and righteous on the outside while their hearts were not committed to the truth of the scripture they supposedly taught. That is, they failed to see Jesus for the savior he was and were leading their people to do the same, thus condemning them all to hell.

The insult still has meaning today, and God still has an awful fate reserved for the wicked snakes who turn their back on Jesus.

It's been so tough this year. We've been snake bitten. I have to thank my fans for helping me get through it.
-- Kyle Busch after his first 2008 Nationwide Series win

Snakes are the "almost" Christians,
the ones for whom faithfulness
is a show that doesn't reach their hearts.

A HOLLYWOOD ENDING

Read Luke 24:1-12.

"Why do you look for the living among the dead? He is not here; he has risen!" (vv. 5, 6a)

Junior Johnson's win at Daytona in 1960 was so improbable that even Hollywood wouldn't touch it because nobody would believe it. Besides, they'd have to name it *Gone with the Wind* and that's already taken.

Without a ride, Johnson didn't even plan to enter. Then eight days before the race he was approached about driving a 1959 Chevrolet that could be converted into a race car if Johnson would agree to drive it. He hesitated because he knew that "the Chevrolets in that era were woefully underpowered, particularly next to the big Pontiacs, and he didn't want to go into the race just to ride around."

But he agreed and when he began practice, he made a discovery that changed stock car racing forever. The Pontiacs inevitably passed him, but he found that if he could latch onto their tail, he could stay with them despite his car's relative lack of power. Johnson had discovered the "bloody black art" of drafting. With some luck, he had a chance to win the race.

A series of crashes eliminated most of the Pontiacs (and 29 of the original field of 68), and Johnson wound up racing Tommy Johns' Pontiac for the win, though Johns appeared uncatchable. Then something incredible and curious happened on lap

192: The back glass suddenly popped out of Johns' car. Johnson said, "I think our speed and the traffic circumstances combined to create a vacuum that sucked that back glass right out." The sudden change in airflow spun Johns out. By the time he righted his car, as Johnson put it, "I was long gone."

To a Hollywood ending nobody would believe.

The world tells us that happy endings are for fairy tales and the movies, that reality is Cinderella dying in childbirth and her prince getting killed in a peasant uprising. But that's just another of the world's lies.

The truth is that Jesus Christ has been producing happy endings for almost two millennia. That's because in Jesus lies the power to change and to rescue a life no matter how desperate the situation. Jesus is the master at putting shattered lives back together, of healing broken hearts and broken relationships, of resurrecting lost dreams.

And as for living happily ever after – God really means it. The greatest Hollywood ending of them all was written on a Sunday morning centuries ago when Jesus left a tomb and death behind. With faith in Jesus, your life can have that same ending. You live with God in peace, joy, and love – forever. The End.

Keep working and try. It'll all eventually work out. If it doesn't so what? You've got to be doing something anyhow.
-- *Dave Marcis*

**Hollywood's happy endings are products
of imagination; the happy endings Jesus produces
are real and are yours for the asking.**

DAY 43

HOW YOU SEE IT

Read John 20:11-18.

"Mary stood outside the tomb crying" (v. 11).

Fans and commentators alike vilified him as being responsible for the most infamous wreck in NASCAR history, but Sterling Marlin came out on the other side of his "season of torment" by keeping his own perspective.

Marlin was the 1983 Winston Cup Series Rookie of the Year. In 1994 and '95, he joined Richard Petty and Cale Yarborough as the only men to win consecutive Daytona 500s.

What has been called Marlin's "long dark ride" began on Feb. 18, 2001, at Daytona when Dale Earnhardt's Chevy and Marlin's Dodge "touched ever so gently." The contact propelled Earnhardt's car up the banking and into the wall, killing him instantly.

NASCAR folk know that wrecks are "one of those racing deals," but this one was different; this was Dale Earnhardt. When Marlin returned home, what he saw on television shocked him. "Some of those media guys who couldn't spell driveshaft . . . [were] saying that I wrecked Earnhardt and put him in the wall," Marlin said.

It wasn't just the media. Threatening phone calls from Earnhardt fans forced Marlin to get an unlisted number. The death threats then came to his race shop via fax. Only when Dale Earnhardt, Jr. issued a statement declaring such behavior by his father's fans "unacceptable" did the furor subside. Earnhardt driver Michael Waltrip also defended him, and a NASCAR investigation into the

NASCAR

accident cleared him of any wrongdoing.

Through it all, Marlin drove exceptionally well, winning two races and finishing a career-best third in the points race. No matter how well he raced, though, he couldn't make people talk about anything other than the wreck.

His manager, Tony Glover, explained how Marlin kept going: "Sterling, in his eyes, realized he didn't do anything wrong." Thus, the threats from the fans were a distraction, but they didn't affect the way he drove.

Your perspective goes a long way toward determining whether you slink through life amid despair, anger, and hopelessness or stride boldly through life with joy and hope. Mary is a good example. On that first Easter morning, she stood by Jesus' tomb crying, her heart broken, because she still viewed everything through the perspective of Jesus' death. But how her attitude, her heart, and her life changed when she saw the morning through the perspective of Jesus' resurrection.

So it is with life and death for all of us. You can't avoid death, but you can determine how you perceive it. Is it fearful, dark, fraught with peril and uncertainty? Or is it a simple little passageway to glory, the light, and loved ones, an elevator ride to paradise?

It's a matter of perspective that depends totally on whether or not you're standing by Jesus' side when it arrives.

Second place is just the first loser.

-- *Dale Earnhardt*

**Whether death is your worst enemy
or a solicitous chauffeur is a matter of perspective.**

CHANCE ENCOUNTER

Read Luke 24:13-35.

"That same day two of them were going to a village. . . .
They were talking with each other about everything that
had happened. . . . Jesus himself came up and walked
along with them" (vv. 13-15).

Benny Parsons is both a driving and an announcing legend who got his start because two guys needed to use the bathroom.

Parsons was named one of NASCAR's 50 Greatest Drivers in 1998 and was inducted into the International Motorsports Hall of Fame in 1994. After retiring from racing in 1988, he became a broadcaster and won an ESPN Emmy in 1996. He appeared as himself in *Talladega Nights: The Ballad of Ricky Bobby.*

Parsons grew up with his great-grandmother in North Carolina without running water or electricity, but that was his choice when his parents moved to Detroit so his father could find work. His dad, Harold, introduced him to racing when Benny visited during the summer.

When he finished high school, Parsons went to Detroit to work for his father, who by now owned a taxicab service and a gas station. "I did whatever it took as far as the mechanical aspects of keeping those cabs running," Parsons said. One day in May 1960, Benny was working at his father's gas station when two men stopped by to use the bathroom. Parson's attention was immediately captured by the race car they had on the back of a truck.

NASCAR

He struck up a conversation by asking the pair where they were headed. He got a reply and a question that set the path for his life: "Anderson, Indiana. Do you want to go?" He did indeed and left immediately. Over the next two years, he traveled with the pair and learned the racing business. His life was changed because of a chance encounter with two men making a pit stop.

Maybe you met your spouse on a blind date or in Kroger's frozen food section. Perhaps a conversation in an elevator or over lunch led to a job offer.

Chance meetings often shape our lives. Some meetings, however, are too important to be left to what seem like the whims of life. If your child is sick, you don't wait until you happen to bump into a physician at Starbuck's to seek help.

So it is with Jesus. Too much is at stake to leave a meeting with him to chance. Instead, you intentionally seek him at church, in the pages of your Bible, on your knees in prayer, or through a conversation with a friend or neighbor. How you conduct the search doesn't matter; what matters is that you find him.

Once you've met him, you should then intentionally cultivate the acquaintance until it is a deep, abiding, life-shaping and life-changing friendship.

It was totally by chance. I happened to be there when that truck stopped only because those guys had to go to the bathroom.
-- Benny Parsons

A meeting with Jesus should not be
one of life's chance encounters, but instead
should be intentionally sought out.

DAY 45

MONKEY BUSINESS

Read Genesis 6:11-22; 8:1-4.

*"God remembered Noah and all the wild animals and the
livestock that were with him in the ark" (v. 8:1).*

For a while, Tim Flock drove with a monkey for a passenger.

Flock was one of the best of the early NASCAR drivers with a
career that ended in 1961 after thirty-nine wins. He was also one
of the sport's greatest characters. He once found himself at a track
with a car that clearly wouldn't cut it. He spotted a new Buick,
which he knew had a powerful V-8 engine, in the parking lot and
asked the owners if he could borrow it for the race. They obliged
and he finished third.

Flock worked on a shoestring in the early days. Since racers
ran on regular street tires, Flock would buy a set from the local
Sears store, race with them, and then return them the next day
with most of the tread scrubbed off. He claimed the tires didn't
deliver the advertised mileage, and he got a replacement set for
his next race. Until the Sears manager caught on.

But his exploits with Jocko Flocko remain one of NASCAR's
oddest stunts. Jocko was a rhesus monkey that rode with Flock in
eight races. He had his own driver's uniform and a special seat.
Evidently appreciating the publicity garnered by the unusual
pair, NASCAR never objected.

Jocko himself, however, was the one who put an end to his
racing days. At Raleigh, Jocko amused himself during the race by

NASCAR

opening a trap door that drivers used to check their tire wear. A pebble flew into the car and socked Jocko on the head. He went berserk, forcing Flock to pit. He said after the race "it was the first time in NASCAR history that a car had to pit to put a monkey out of it." And the last time too.

You probably don't have a monkey riding with you in the car, but you may well have a dog or two around the place. How about a cat that passes time staring longingly at your caged canary? Kids have gerbils? Maybe you've gone more exotic with a tarantula or a ferret.

Americans love our pets; in fact, more households in this country have pets than have children. We not only share our living space with animals we love and protect but also with some – such as roaches and rats – that we seek to exterminate.

None of us, though, has the problems Noah faced when he packed God's menagerie into one boat. God saved all his varmints from extinction, including the fish and the ducks, who were probably quite delighted with the whole flood business.

The lesson is clear for we who strive to live as God would have us: All living things are under God's care. God doesn't call us to care for and respect just our beloved pets; we are to serve God as stewards of all of his creatures.

I've always had a love for dogs, just wanted to play with them out in the yard, roll around out in the grass and go do things with them.
-- Ryan Newman

God cares about all his creatures,
and he expects us to respect them too

THE SIMPLE LIFE

Read 1 John 1:5-10.

"If we confess our sins, he is faithful and just and will forgive us our sins and purify us from all unrighteousness" (v. 9).

You would think that the winningest driver in NASCAR history, a man so successful and so recognized that he has been dubbed the sport's "King," would have a complex formula to explain his accomplishments. Not in Richard Petty's case.

Petty in fact always kept it simple with his "humble wisdom and no-frills, down-home philosophy." What's been called his "feet-on-the-floor royalty," which never let him get carried away with himself, explained the devotion of his fans. He is credited with being the first driver to promote driver-fan friendliness. The King mingled with his subjects by consistently going over to fences after races to sign autographs, chat, and smile.

The wins came for Petty like no other driver in NASCAR history, a record 200 of them in a career that began in 1958 and ended with his retirement in 1992. He won the Daytona 500 a record seven times; Dale Earnhardt and he are the only two drivers to win the Cup championship seven times. In 1967 he dominated as no driver ever had before or has since, winning 27 races, including ten in a row at one stretch. He is widely considered the greatest NASCAR driver of all time.

"My object was to win," Petty once declared. And so what was the formula behind all those wins and all that success? Like Petty himself, it's straightforward: "Get from Turn One to Turn Two to Turn Three to the checkered flag. That's what it's all about," he explained.

Perhaps the simple life in America was doomed by the arrival of the programmable VCR. Since then, we've been on an inevitably downward spiral into ever more complicated lives. Even windshield wipers have multiple settings now, and it takes a graduate degree to figure out clothes dryers.

But we might do well in our own lives to mimic the simple formula Richard Petty employed. That is, we should approach our lives with the keen awareness that success requires simplicity, a sticking to the basics: Revere God, love our families, honor our country, do our best.

Theologians may make what God did in Jesus as complicated as quantum mechanics and the infield fly rule, but God kept it simple for us: believe, trust, and obey. Believe in Jesus as the Son of God, trust that through him God makes possible our deliverance from our sins into Heaven, and obey God in the way he wants us to live. It's simple, but it's the true winning formula, the way to win for all eternity.

First you learn to drive fast. Next, you learn to drive fast in traffic. Then you learn how to do it for 500 miles.
                                                      -- Alan Kulwicki

**Life continues to get ever more complicated,
but God made faith simple for us
when he showed up as Jesus.**

DREAM WORLD

Read Joel 2:26-28.

"Your old men will dream dreams, your young men will see visions" (v. 28).

He was universally recognized as one of the greatest crew chiefs ever -- and he suddenly walked away from it.

Kirk Shelmerdine was only 29 when he was inducted into the International Mechanics Hall of Fame in 1987. This was merely the placing of a formal stamp onto what everybody in racing already knew. In 1983, he became the youngest crew chief in history to win a Winston Cup race, but he topped that when he was 28 by becoming the youngest crew chief in history to win a Winston Cup championship.

As David Poole and Jim McLaurin put it in *"Then Junior Said to Jeff . . .,"* "Shelmerdine was cut from special cloth, and the combination of [Dale] Earnhardt, [Richard] Childress, and himself could have won more titles." In 1992, though, Shelmerdine walked away from his crew chief duties and basically started over. Why would he do such a thing?

He had a dream to pursue. Back in 1981, he went South from Pennsylvania to be a driver, not a crew chief, and that dream got put on hold. Being a driver "was my motivation for getting into racing," Shelmerdine said. "I always had that kind of desire in me. I was wired for it."

After saying good-bye to the big money, he opened his own

shop down the street from the Childress operation in Welcome, N.C., with an "annual budget that would not have covered the expenses of one race with his old team."

Shelmerdine never matched the success behind the wheel he had had under the hood, but that didn't matter. He was happier chasing his dream.

You have dreams. Maybe to make a lot of money. Write the great American novel. Or have the fairy-tale romance. But dreams often are crushed beneath the weight of everyday living; reality, not dreams, comes to occupy your time, attention, and effort. You've come to understand that achieving your dreams requires a combination of persistence, timing, and providence.

But what if your dreams don't come true because they're not good enough? That is, they're based on the alluring but totally unreliable promises of the world rather than the true promises of God, which are a sure thing.

God calls us to great achievements because God's dreams for us are greater than our dreams for ourselves. Such greatness occurs, though, only when our dreams and God's will for our lives are the same. Your dreams should be worthy of your best – and worthy of God's involvement in making them come true.

I'm a full-blooded racer. For me to be able to live a dream tickles me pink.

                                                      -- Joe Nemechek

**Dreams based on the world's promises
are often crushed; those based on God's promises
are a sure thing.**

DAY 48

FACING THE MUSIC

Read Psalm 98.

"Sing to the Lord a new song, for he has done marvelous things" (v. 1).

If stock-car racing had a P.T. Barnum, it would be Howard Augustine 'Humpy' Wheeler."

What have been called Wheeler's "vast contributions to racing" came as a promoter and track president. He was inducted into the International Motorsports Hall of Fame in 2006. As president of Lowe's Motor Speedway, Wheeler's genius for publicity stunts asserted itself. His philosophy as a race promoter was that his job was "to provide a little 'Technicolor' for people who lead black-and-white lives."

Once he provided that Technicolor after he overheard two sportswriters griping about his "lavish pre-race extravaganzas. 'They might as well have a circus,' one said. The next year, the pre-race show was, literally, a circus."

After Cale Yarborough slapped the less-than-complimentary nickname "Jaws" on rival Darrell Waltrip, Wheeler bought a giant dead shark, placed a dead chicken in its mouth, and had it driven around the track on a flatbed trailer before a race. Yarborough's sponsor then was Holly Farms Poultry.

All of Wheeler's ideas didn't necessarily pan out. For a Coca-Cola 600 in the 1980s, he announced that as part of his "lavish pre-race extravaganza," he would assemble the largest band in history. Dozens of high schools responded to Wheeler's call and sent their bands to the speedway. Unfortunately, the day turned out miserably hot, and "before a note was played, some among the thousands of kids started dropping from heat exhaustion." And they kept falling out. "They were dropping like flies," Wheeler said; he finally and mercifully halted the show.

Maybe you can't play a lick or carry a tune in the proverbial bucket. Or perhaps you do know your way around a guitar or a keyboard and can sing "God Bless America" on karaoke night without closing the joint down or insulting our national honor.

Unless you're a professional musician, however, how well you play or sing really doesn't matter. What counts is that you have music in your heart and sometimes you have to turn it loose.

Worshipping God has always included music in some form. That same boisterous enthusiasm you exhibit at and during a NASCAR race when some of your favorite music plays should be a part of the joy you have in your personal worship of God.

When you consider that God loves you, he always will, and he has arranged through Jesus for you to spend eternity with him, how can that song God put in your heart not burst forth?

The show must go on!
-- Humpy Wheeler as the band kids dropped from heat exhaustion
The show must stop!
-- Humpy Wheeler as the band kids kept dropping

You call it music; others may call it noise;
God calls it praise
when it's played and sung to His glory.

FEAR FACTOR

Read Matthew 14:22-33.

"[The disciples] cried out in fear. But Jesus immediately said to them: 'Take courage! It is I. Don't be afraid'" (vv. 26-27).

It was frightening to competitors and spectators alike. Even to someone like Fireball Roberts." "It" was the brand new Daytona International Speedway.

The track was the vision of NASCAR's ultimate visionary, Bill France, Sr. In 1953, France pondered ways to make NASCAR grow, and he came upon the idea of building bigger tracks with higher banks, longer straightaways, and asphalt surfaces. The result would be cars that would go much faster. He decided to build a superspeedway at Daytona Beach, a track "the likes of which the world of stock car racing had never seen."

The track was finished in 1959, and France staged some events in February at the old beach venue, but they were only lead-ins to the grand finale: a 500-mile race for the biggest purse in stock car racing history.

While France touted the grand and glorious nature of the track's features and its future, others weren't so sure. Many of the drivers, including Roberts, had safety concerns about the high speeds the track would make possible -- and necessary. When Max Muhleman of the *Charlotte News* visited the track for the first time, he thought, "These guys will never survive this track. . . . It was an awesome thing."

The initial Daytona 500 was run on Feb. 22, 1959. In a photo finish, Johnny Beauchamp was declared the winner before Lee Petty was announced the winner sixty-one hours after the race was over. About running that frightful track on that historic day, Petty said, "There wasn't a man there who wasn't scared to death of it."

Some fears are universal; others are particular. Speaking to the Rotary Club may require a heavy dose of antiperspirant. Elevator walls may feel as though they're closing in on you. And don't even get started on being in the dark with spiders and snakes during a thunderstorm.

We all live in fear, and God knows this. Dozens of passages in the Bible urge us not to be afraid. God isn't telling us to lose our wariness of oncoming cars or big dogs with nasty dispositions; this is a helpful fear God instilled in us for protection.

What God does wish driven from our lives is a spirit of fear that dominates us, that makes our lives miserable and keeps us from doing what we should, such as sharing our faith. In commanding that we not be afraid, God reminds us that when we trust completely in him, we find peace that calms our fears.

Other tracks separate the men from the boys. Daytona will separate the brave from the weak after the boys are gone.
                                   -- Jimmy Thompson just prior to Daytona's opening

You have your own peculiar set of fears,
but they should never paralyze you
because God is greater than anything you fear.

THE SCARS

Read John 20:19-31.

'"Put your finger here; see my hands. Reach out your
hand and put it into my side. Stop doubting and believe'"
(v. 27).

The story spread that Joe Weatherly got his scar from a German sniper's bullet while he was in the Army in World War II -- but the truth was much more grisly and much more tragic.

Weatherly enjoyed a successful twelve-year NASCAR career that ended with his death in an accident at Riverside Road Course in January 1964. He won 25 races, placed in the top five 105 times, and won the points championship in 1962 and '63.

He raced with a scar described as "a long straightaway down the left side of his face. It ran shallow across his forehead and sliced through his eyelids and dug deep into his cheek." He got that scar in a wreck that killed one man and nearly killed him.

In October 1946 in Norfolk, Va., Weatherly's Buick jumped a curb and hit a tree head-on. He was "hung up in the broken windshield, his face cleaved in two." As Norfolk policeman Charles Grant put it, Weatherly had been cut "all the way down the face and into his jugular vein." He was bleeding so profusely that "he'd have died in a few more minutes."

An off-duty policeman clamped his hands over Weatherly's neck until an ambulance arrived, saving his life. While officers said speed was the culprit in the awful wreck, Weatherly argued otherwise, noting that before the wreck, he had stopped only a block away from the crash site to say hello to a friend. Jean Flanagan, who had both legs broken in the accident and who married Weatherly in 1948, said that the collision with the curb broke the steering rod "and the tree was right there."

Weatherly was left with a permanent reminder of the awful night in Norfolk.

You've got scars too. Maybe like Joe Weatherly, a car wreck left a good one. So did that bicycle crash. Maybe we better not talk about that time you said, "Hey, watch this!" Your scars are part of your life story, the residue of the pain you've encountered. People's scars are so unique and ubiquitous they're used to identify bodies.

Even Jesus proved who he was by the scars of the nail marks in his hands and his side. How interesting it is that even after his resurrection, Jesus bore the scars of the pain he endured. Apparently, he bears them still even as he sits upon his throne in Heaven. Why would he even have them in the first place? Why would he, who had all the power in the universe, submit meekly to being tortured and slaughtered?

He did it for you. Jesus' scars tell the story of his love for you.

Joe Weatherly's scar crossed his mouth so that when he grinned, as Joe was predisposed to do, he left a third of the smile behind.
-- Writer Earl Swift

In your scars lie stories; the same is true for Jesus, whose scars tell of His love for you.

PRESSURE COOKER

Read 1 Kings 18:16-40.

"Answer me, O Lord, answer me, so these people will know that you, O Lord, are God" (v. 37).

Joe Nemechek described the pressure on NASCAR drivers as "immense." In today's high-stakes sport where the rewards are great but the risks are greater, Nemechek is right. So imagine a driver being so calm and relaxed during the closing laps of a race he's leading that he takes his hands off the wheel to grab a drink of water!

That's what Tony Stewart did during the Allstate 400 on July 29, 2007. Stewart was the Sprint Cub Series champion in 2002, edging Mark Martin by 38 points, and in 2005, besting Greg Biffle by 35 points. He was the first and only driver to win championships in stock cars, Indy cars, and open-wheel Midget, Sprint and Silver Crown cars.

That July afternoon at the Brickyard, Stewart had a comfortable lead when ESPN cut to an in-car camera view and caught him at his relaxed best. "While everyone behind him was jockeying to achieve the best finish they could, Stewart casually reached for a water bottle and took a long gulp." In the process, he took both hands off the wheel "and effortlessly drove down the front stretch with the steering wheel wedged between his knees."

Pressure? What pressure?

Here was Stewart just a couple of laps from the finish line, "treating what likely will be the second-biggest race win in his career" just as casually as you please. He drove as though he didn't have a care in the world, which, writer Jerry Bonkowski said, is when Stewart is at his best, noting that's exactly the way Stewart drove to the championship in 2005. "He didn't fret, didn't worry and didn't waver."

On this day, Stewart simply went for a Sunday afternoon drive, quenching his thirst along the way.

You live every day with pressure. As Elijah did so long ago, you lay it on the line with everybody watching. Your family, coworkers, or employees – they depend on you. You know the pressure of a deadline, of a job evaluation, of taking the risk of asking someone to go out with you, of driving in rush-hour traffic.

Help in dealing with daily pressure is readily available, and the only price you pay for it is your willingness to believe. God will give you the grace to persevere if you ask prayerfully.

And while you may need some convincing, the pressures of daily living are really small potatoes because they all will pass. The real pressure comes in deciding where you will spend eternity because that decision is forever. You can handle that pressure easily enough by deciding for Jesus. Eternity is then taken care of; the pressure's off – forever.

Nobody puts more pressure on me to perform than myself.
-- Jimmie Johnson

**The greatest pressure you face in life
concerns where you spend eternity,
which can be handled by deciding for Jesus.**

HANGING IN THERE

Read Mark 14:32-42.

"'Father,' he said, 'everything is possible for you. Take this cup from me. Yet not what I will, but what you will'" (v. 36).

Tiny Lund's persistence snared him the love of his life.

In 1968 at a race in Columbia, S.C., DeWayne Louis Lund met a little 19-year-old farm girl named Wanda from North Carolina. For Tiny, it was love at first sight; for Wanda, it was much less. "I was not at all excited about meeting Tiny," Wanda said. "If I was to meet a real race car driver, I wanted to meet Buck Baker."

When their paths crossed a second time at a race in Rockingham, he announced she should give him her phone number "right now because I am going to marry you." "Honey," Wanda replied, "my momma would kill me if I dragged someone like you home." What turned her off was how big Lund was (six foot five, 250 pounds). "I was thinking, I'm five foot two, and there ain't no way in your wildest dreams."

Undeterred, Lund called her repeatedly and asked her for dates until finally Wanda realized she had to let him know exactly where he stood loud and clear. She made a date and stood him up. "I was terrible, awful, figuring that sooner or later he'd get the message." But he didn't listen very well.

Lund just "happened" to show up at a lake where Wanda was learning to ski. She had a ski belt on, and Lund urged her to wear a vest since she couldn't swim and sometimes the belts broke. She ignored him, thinking to herself, "Who do you think you are?"

Sure enough, her belt broke and she sank like a rock. Lund jumped in and pulled her out choking and sputtering. He gave her a good shaking, turned her over his knee, and spanked her like a two-year old for not listening to him. After that, they dated and married and were together until the day he died, all because Tiny Lund was persistent.

Life is tough; it inevitably beats us up and kicks us around some. But life has four quarters, and so here we are, still standing, still in the game. We know that we can never win if we don't finish. We emerge as winners and champions only if we never give up, if we just see it through.

Interestingly, Jesus has been in the same situation. On that awful night in the garden, Jesus understood the nature of the suffering he was about to undergo, and he begged God to take it from him. In the end, though, he yielded to God's will and surrendered his own.

Even in the matter of persistence, Jesus is our example. As he did, we push doggedly and determinedly ahead – following God's will for our lives -- no matter how hard it gets. And we can do it because God is with us.

To finish first, you must first finish.

-- *Rick Mears*

**It's tough to keep going no matter what,
but you have the power of almighty God
to pull you through.**

WORK ETHIC

Read Matthew 9:35-38.

"Then he said to his disciples, 'The harvest is plentiful but the workers are few. Ask the Lord of the harvest, therefore, to send out workers into his harvest field'" (vv. 37-38).

Juanita Epton was present for more than fifty runnings of the Daytona 500, but she never saw a race. She had work to do.

Epton's first experience with racing came in 1945 when her husband, Joe, parked her on a hill close to the action of a dirt track in Charlotte. "When the race was over," Epton said, "my entire body had been covered by that red-clay dust. I was so angry, I said I would never go near another race."

But she did, joining Joe in the move to Daytona when Bill France opened the speedway in 1958. Joe had begun working for France in 1945 as an official scorer, timer, and carpenter. For more than fifty years, she worked in the speedway's ticket office that Joe built. She admitted the speedway became "a second home. This has always been a great place to work."

While she met presidents and astronauts and counted many of the drivers among her friends, she never tolerated bending of the rules by anyone. She once scolded the speedway's president, telling him his SUV was too big to be parked beside her minivan in the employee parking lot. "I wasn't about to mess with her," he said, promptly finding another spot.

Epton started out logging ticket sales in notepads and then

counting them by hand, admittedly "working my fingers to the bone in those early years." She eventually made the transition to computers. Only rarely did she ever sneak a peek at the action. "I always felt it was my duty to be [in the ticket office]," she said. "I'm a fan of the sport, but if I want to sit down and enjoy a race, I'll go to another track."

When Dale Earnhardt was killed in 2001, she cried. But she did what she always did: She kept working.

Do you embrace hard work or try to avoid it? No matter how hard you may try, you really can't escape hard work. Funny thing about all these labor-saving devices like cell phones and laptop computers: You're working longer and harder than ever. For many of us, our work defines us perhaps more than any other aspect of our lives. But there's a workforce you're a part of that doesn't show up in any Labor Department statistics or any IRS records.

You're part of God's staff; God has a specific job that only you can do for him. It's often referred to as a "calling," but it amounts to your serving God where there is a need in the way that best suits your God-given abilities and talents

You should stand ready to work for God all the time, 24-7. Those are awful hours, but the benefits are out of this world.

Why did I take up racing? I was too lazy to work and too chicken to steal.

-- *Kyle Petty*

**God calls you to work for him using the talents
and gifts he gave you; whether you're a worker
or a malingerer is up to you.**

THE TESTING TIME

Read James 1:2-12.

"Blessed is the man who perseveres under trial, because when he has stood the test, he will receive the crown of life that God has promised to those who love him" (v. 12).

Ford gave Benny Parsons an assignment that was ridiculous and impossible, and it changed his life.

In December 1967, Parsons was running in the ARCA series when Ford invited him to a party and he found himself at a shindig that included Mario Andretti and A.J. Foyt. "I didn't know why I had been invited to the party," Parsons said. "I didn't know why my name was on the list."

He found out why a short time later when a Ford official called him and told him they had a car for him to race at Daytona if he would pick it up and put the engine together. Working at his dad's gas station with a two-year-old child, Parsons was in no position to turn down this opportunity.

But what they gave him was "a frame with a body hung on it. No doors, no fenders, no hoods. They [took] everything from the car and threw it in my truck and said, 'Here you go.' We had never seen a car like that before. I didn't have the first clue how to fix it up," he said. When he pulled into Detroit with the thing, he was told, "This is ridiculous. You need to call them up and tell them you can't make it. You can't do it."

But Parsons realized something: "This was a test to see how

badly I wanted to race. How do you test someone? You back them up to the wall and give them an impossible task. That's what they did to me. It was an impossible task."

He had twenty-one days to build an engine and get the car ready. He scoured local junkyards for parts and worked practically all the time putting his ride together in a wooden garage behind a friend's house.

He made it to Daytona in his makeshift car and sat on the pole for the ARCA race. Parsons had been tested and was on his way.

Life often seems to be one battery of tests after another: high-school and college final exams, college entrance exams, the driver's license test, professional certification exams. They all stress us out because they measure our competency, and we fear that we will be found wanting.

But it is the tests in our lives that don't involve paper and pen that often demand the most of us. That is, like Benny Parsons, we regularly run headlong into challenges, obstacles, and barriers that test our abilities, our persistence, and our faith.

Life itself is one long test, which means some parts are bound to be hard. Viewing life as an ongoing exam may help you keep your sanity, your perspective, and your faith when troubles come your way. After all, God is the proctor, but he isn't neutral. He even gave you the answer you need to pass with flying colors; that answer is "Jesus."

The impossible just took a little more determination, but we got it done.
-- *Benny Parsons*

Life is a test that God wants you to ace.

FOOD FOR THOUGHT

Read Genesis 9:1-7.

"Everything that lives and moves will be food for you. Just as I gave you the green plants, I now give you everything" (v. 3).

Nutritionists in the pits? Salmon instead of a New York strip? Moon Pies banned? It's outrageous! In today's NASCAR, though, many drivers have come to consider diet and nutrition crucial to their careers.

And to their health. Kim Severson wrote, "Toward the end of a race, after three muscle-tense hours in a cockpit that reaches 120 degrees, dehydration saps concentration and poorly fed muscles fail. At 190 miles an hour, the wrong dish at lunch or one quart too few of water could mean, quite literally, death."

Still, spiral pasta and sweet potatoes are not what most folks think of when they think of NASCAR foods. As Darrell Waltrip put it, "I ran a lot, but I certainly didn't pay attention to what I ate. Most of it was fried, and I'm a Southern boy, so if you can fry it, I'll eat it."

But change is clearly here. Jeff Gordon loved his fast food and corn dogs until he realized both his body and his career would be better served with a more healthful diet. While he still sneaks in an occasional steak and a bowl of rocky road ice cream and could always eat a whole jar of green olives or pickles, Gordon admitted, "I used to hate salmon. Now I love it."

NASCAR

Not everyone has shied away from the chow wagon. For instance, Tony Stewart once had his seat redesigned to account for his extra weight. And while Brian Vickers worked with a nutritionist, he still scarfed down his favorite breakfast: three scrambled eggs, seven slices of bacon, and white bread with grape jelly. Plus an occasional frozen pepperoni pizza.

Belly up to the buffet, boys and girls, for barbecue, sirloin steak, grilled chicken, and fried catfish with hush puppies and cheese grits. Rachael Ray's a household name; hamburger joints, pizza parlors, and taco stands lurk on every corner; and we have a TV channel devoted exclusively to food. We love our chow.

Food is one of God's really good ideas, but consider the complex divine plan that begins with a seed and ends with French fries. The creator of all life devised a system in which living things are sustained and nourished physically through the sacrifice of other living things in a way similar to what Christ underwent to save us spiritually.

Whether it's fast food or home-cooked, everything we eat is a gift from God secured through a divine plan in which some plants and animals have given up their lives.

Pausing to give thanks before we dive in seems the least we can do.

Basically we NASCAR fans will eat anything, and we're proud of it.
-- Chef and NASCAR fan Mario Batali

God created a system that nourishes you
through the sacrifice of other living things;
that's worth a thank-you.

YOUNG BLOOD

Read: Jeremiah 1:4-10.

"The Lord said to me, 'Do not say, 'I am only a child' . . .
for I am with you and will rescue you" (vv. 7a, 8).

Over the years, NASCAR has not been a sport that looked upon young drivers too kindly.

On the track, experience has traditionally counted as much as talent. In 1972, rookie Darrell Waltrip, 25, created a stir by leading for seven laps in only his fourth Grand National race. At the time, no one could recall a rookie ever leading a superspeedway race before. Still, Waltrip needed three more years and 49 tries to win his first NASCAR race. In an earlier age, "You had to prove yourself before you got a chance to make it," recalled Mark Martin.

Recent history backs up an assessment that today's NASCAR is about younger drivers. Dale Jarrett was 31 when he raced his first full Cup season; Bobby Labonte was 29, Dale Earnhardt 27. In 1996, only three fulltime NASCAR drivers were younger than 30: Jeff Gordon, Jeremy Mayfield, and Jeff Burton. Even then, though, a youth movement was stirring in NASCAR. By 2006, sixteen full-time Nextel Cup drivers were younger than 30.

They were also being successful. Gordon was an unheard-of 21 when he began his first Cup season in 1993. By the time he was 27, he had 42 wins and three championships. In September 2005, Kyle Busch became the youngest driver ever to win a Cup race; he was 20. His brother, Kurt, won the Cup title in 2004; he was 26.

Dale Earnhardt, Jr. was 25 when he won his first Cup races. Carl Edwards won four Cup races at 26. In 2003, Brian Vickers, at the ripe old age of 20, won the Busch title to become the youngest national series champion in NASCAR history

Why the change? Many younger guys can flat-out drive as their record proves. Also, today's corporate culture demands younger drivers to promote their products. As never before in NASCAR, youth will be served.

While the media seem inordinately obsessed with youth, most aspects of our society value experience and some hard-won battle scars. Life usually requires us to spend time on the bench as a reserve, waiting for our chance to play with the big boys and girls. You probably rode some pine in high school. You started college as a lowly freshman. You began work at an entry-level position. Even head football coaches learn their trade as assistants.

Paying your dues is traditional, but that shouldn't stop you from doing something bold right away, as today's younger NASCAR drivers are doing. Nowhere is this truer than in your faith life.

You may well assert that you are too young and too inexperienced to really do anything for God. Those are just excuses, however, and God won't pay a lick of attention to them when he issues a call. After all, the younger you are, the more time you have to serve.

When I came up, Cup owners didn't want young guys. They wanted veterans with judgment. That's not the way it is anymore.

-- *Mark Martin*

**Youth is no excuse for not serving God;
it just gives you more time.**

LANGUAGE BARRIER

Read Acts 2:1-21.

"Divided tongues, as of fire, appeared among them, and a tongue rested on each of them. All of them were filled with the Holy Spirit and began to speak in other languages, as the Spirit gave them ability" (vv. 3-4 NRSV).

You would think two guys from Kentucky and North Carolina wouldn't have a problem communicating, but for Junior Johnson and Darrell Waltrip, that once wasn't the case.

David Poole and Jim McLaurin relate in *"Then Junior Said to Jeff . . ."* the story of the first time Waltrip went into Johnson's shop as a new driver. Waltrip wanted to make a good impression, so he pestered Johnson to give him something to do. Johnson didn't really have anything, but he found something.

According to Waltrip, Johnson told him, "Go out there and bounce them tires." Waltrip explained that "to seat the tires on the wheel, you would take the tires and bounce them so the tire would go out against the wheel and not leak."

So that's what Waltrip did with about 40 tires Johnson had in the yard -- sort of. Waltrip admitted, "I didn't know how to do it, but I'd seen guys do it." So he bounced a tire -- and off it went right on down the hill. "Another one bounced off a guy's car. I had tires everywhere."

Johnson walked out and disgustedly eyed the mayhem. "Get them tires gathered up," he barked at Waltrip. "Get over there to the machine and get them tires bounced like I told you." With the mention of the machine, Waltrip realized Johnson had instructed him to "balance" the tires, not bounce them.

Racing translates easily across national and cultural boundaries, but as Junior Johnson's and Darrell Waltrip's humorous problem illustrates, language often erects a real barrier to understanding. Recall your overseas vacation or your call to a tech support number when you got someone who spoke English but didn't understand it. Talking loud and waving your hands doesn't facilitate communication; it just makes you look weird.

Like many other aspects of life, faith has its jargon that can sometimes hinder understanding. Sanctification, justification, salvation, Advent, Communion with its symbolism of eating flesh and drinking blood – these and many other words have specific meanings to Christians that may be incomprehensible, confusing, and downright daunting to the newcomer or the seeker.

But the heart of Christianity's message centers on words that require no explanation: words such as hope, joy, love, purpose, and community. Their meanings are universal because people the world over seek them in their lives.

Nobody speaks that language better than Jesus.

Every one of these drivers in the garage area, I can speak to because they all speak English, [except for] Ward Burton. He speaks Ward.
-- *Tony Stewart*

Jesus speaks across all language barriers
because his message of hope and meaning
resounds with people everywhere.

MIRACLE PLAY

Read Matthew 12:38-42.

"He answered, 'A wicked and adulterous generation asks for a miraculous sign!'" (v. 39)

When your driver doesn't respond, you get a really sick feeling." So spoke crew chief Larry McReynolds about the afternoon of August 19, 1994.

His driver was Ernie Irvan, and he had crashed head-on into a wall at Michigan. "I called and called and called, 'Ernie, are you OK? Ernie, are you OK?' And he wasn't responding."

When McReynolds approached Irvan's car on turn two, a rescue worker told him, "You don't want to go over there." But McReynolds did -- and his response was to throw up. "It looked like a bucket of blood had been poured there," he said. There where his best friend sat. McReynolds said he thought, "It can't be possible."

Writer Peter Golenbock called it The Ernie Irvan Miracle -- that afternoon when Irvan was hurt so badly that McReynolds prayed for God to take Irvan to Heaven rather than have him suffer and be comatose. The doctors gave Irvan less than a twenty percent chance of surviving.

But he made it. Five days after the crash, Irvan's chances for survival were getting better. Two weeks after the accident, McReynolds walked into Irvan's room and couldn't believe what he saw. "It was phenomenal," he said. The thoughts of those who knew Irvan began to turn from whether he would survive to whether he would drive again.

By the end of 1994, Irvin had declared, "I'm going to race." In the late summer of 1995, Irvan drove onto the track at North Wilkesboro to qualify. McReynolds said of the miraculous moment, "I thought those people were going to rip the grandstand down." And when Irvan qualified, the miracle was complete.

Miracles – like Ernie Irvan's survival and return to racing -- defy rational explanation. Or like recovering from an illness that seemed terminal. Underlying the notion of miracles is that they are rare instances of direct divine intervention that reveal God.

But life shows us quite the contrary, that miracles are anything but rare. Since God made the world and everything in it, everything around you is miraculous. Even you are a miracle.

Your life therefore can be mundane, dull, and ordinary, or it can be spent in a glorious attitude of childlike wonder and awe. It depends on whether or not you see the world through the eyes of faith. Only through faith can you discern the hand of God in any event; only through faith can you see the miraculous and thus see God.

Jesus knew that miracles don't produce faith, but rather faith produces miracles.

No one would ever say there isn't a God on this earth if they knew what went on in that three-week period of time [after Ernie Irvan's wreck].
                                                                    -- Larry McReynolds

**Miracles are all around us,
but it takes the eyes of faith to see them.**

WATER POWER

Read Acts 10:34-48.

"Can anyone keep these people from being baptized with water? They have received the Holy Spirit just as we have" (v. 47).

When Janet Guthrie made her NASCAR debut at the World 600 in Charlotte at Lowe's Motorspeedway in 1976, rookie track promoter Humpy Wheeler learned a valuable lesson about women, bathrooms, and water.

Guthrie qualified 27th, and suddenly what had begun as a publicity stunt became a historical event. As Wheeler put it, "We're talking about 1976. This was not a woman competing just in a sports event. This was really a sociological revolution that was going on." Never before had a woman qualified for a race on a high-banked superspeedway or driven a race of this length. Gurthie had to change into her uniform in the spectators' area because there were no women's restrooms in the garage.

The day after Guthrie made the field, Wheeler said the track had its greatest one-day ticket sales in history. More than 100,000 people were at the track that day, about 10,000 more than the previous record. Wheeler saw something he had never seen before: taxis bringing people to the track. The taxis in most cases had only one passenger, a woman.

Gurthrie finished 15th, one lap off the pace but ahead of the likes of Dale Earnhardt and Bill Elliott.

NASCAR

Wheeler learned a vital lesson that day about running a track: Women use more water in a restroom than men do. With the unusual number of women present, the track ran out of water halfway through the race. The track temperature exceeded one hundred degrees and the biggest crowd in the track's history was present, so Wheeler had a real emergency on his hands. He frantically coerced the local volunteer fire departments to speed to the track and empty their trucks.

Children's wading pools and swimming pools in the backyard. Fishing, boating, skiing, and swimming at a lake. Sun, sand, and surf at the beach. If there's any water around, we'll probably be in it, on it, or near it. If there's not any at hand, we'll build a dam and create our own.

We love the wet stuff for its recreational uses, but water first and foremost is about its absolute necessity to support and maintain life. From its earliest days, the Christian church appropriated water as an image of life through the ritual of baptism. Since the time of the arrival of the Holy Spirit at Pentecost, baptism with water has been the symbol of entry into the Christian community. It is water that marks a person as belonging to Jesus. It is through water that a person proclaims that Jesus is his Lord.

There's something in the water, all right. There is life.

I thought it was a nuclear explosion because there were fire trucks coming from 360 points flying in here with their sirens going.
-- Humpy Wheeler describing fire trucks delivering water to the track

There is life in the water:
physical life and spiritual life.

BODY LANGUAGE

Read 1 Corinthians 6:12-20.

*"Do you not know that your body is a temple of the Holy
Spirit, who is in you, whom you have received from God?
... Honor God with your body" (vv. 19, 20b).*

Today's Lowe's Motor Speedway in Charlotte is one of the great
gems of NASCAR, but back when it opened in 1960 for its first
race, it was a disaster.

The superspeedway was the brainchild of driver Curtis Turner
and longtime race promoter Bruton Smith. It opened on June 19,
1960, way over budget and almost a month late; it also wasn't
ready for a race. The asphalt hadn't had time to cure, and each
time cars took to the track, they dug up huge chunks that flew
everywhere. As Joe Menzer put it, "The more Turner and Smith
tried to fix the problems, the worse they seemed to get." A writer
called the track "a bumpy asphalt quilt."

The night before the race, eight hundred tons of asphalt were
removed and replaced on the track, covered by two thousand
gallons of liquid rubber sealer. That didn't exactly encourage the
drivers.

Lured by the record purse, though, they raced anyhow. Fearing
they would spend the day dodging chunks of asphalt, crews put
bars and chicken wire on the windshields and fender flaps behind
the rear wheels. One writer said, "The front of the cars resembled
a steam locomotive cowcatcher." All the precautions didn't matter.

NASCAR

"The asphalt broke apart and holes developed, causing broken axles, wheels, bearings and differentials and blown tires."

Late in the race, Jack Smith was leading by five laps when he was undone by a chunk of flying asphalt that ruptured his gas tank. His crew gamely tried to salvage the day by stuffing rags into the hole, but the track had finished him.

Your body may never have given you the problems the Lowe's speedway did back in 1960, but most of us still don't see a body beautiful when we look into a mirror. We may well see only "a bumpy asphalt quilt." Too heavy, too short, too pale, too gray, and where'd all the hair go? We often compare ourselves to an impossible standard Hollywood and fashion magazines have created, and we are inevitably disappointed.

God must have been quite partial to your body, though, because he personally fashioned it and gave it to you free of charge. Your body, like everything else in your life, is thus a gift from God. But God didn't stop there. He then quite voluntarily chose to inhabit your body, sharing it with you in the person of the Holy Spirit.

What an act of consummate ungratefulness it is then to abuse your God-given body by violating God's standards for living. To do so is in fact to dishonor God.

I don't believe anybody could finish this race in a tank.
-- Fireball Roberts after he qualified for the first race at what would become Lowe's Motor Speedway

You may not have a fine opinion of your body,
but God thought enough of it
to personally create it for you.

DAY 61

ROCK SOLID

Read Luke 6:46-49.

"I will show you what he is like who comes to me and hears my words and puts them into practice. He is like a man building a house, who dug down deep and laid the foundation on rock" (vv. 47-48).

Gambling and lying are not exactly the foundations on which to build a worthwhile, constructive life.

On April 12, 2008, however, Jimmie Johnson used a little of both to win the Subway Fresh Pit 500 at Phoenix International Speedway. Johnson took the gamble; Chad Knaus, his crew chief, told the lie that helped the gamble pay off.

Johnson was among the leaders when they all pitted with 82 laps to go. At that point, conventional wisdom said that everyone would need one more pit stop and that at least one more caution would come. The latter never happened, and that's where Johnson's gamble came in.

The Hendrick Motorsports team made a crucial decision as the leaders dove for the pits to take on gas in the waning laps. Johnson and Knaus stayed on the track, gambling they would have enough fuel to finish. Part of that decision on Johnson's part was based on Knaus' little white lie. He kept telling his driver he had a solid 20-second lead on Clint Bowyer, the only other driver who elected not to pit. That meant Johnson could slow down a little to conserve fuel. The truth was that he had only about a

10-second lead.

Johnson admitted his instinct was to step on the gas, so Knaus' lie helped them stretch their fuel. Was Knaus worried? "Yeah, the whole run," he said.

Your life is much like a race on race day; it's an ongoing project, a work in progress. As it is, though, with any complex construction job, if your life is to be stable, it must have a solid foundation. Otherwise, like a NASCAR driver who can't recover from a heartbreaking loss, your life runs out of gas at the first trouble that comes your way.

R. Alan Culpepper said in *The New Interpreter's Bible*, "We do not choose whether we will face severe storms in life; we only get to choose the foundation on which we will stand." In other words, tough times are inevitable. If your foundation isn't rock-solid, you will have nothing on which to stand as those storms buffet you, nothing to keep your life from flying apart into a cycle of disappointment and destruction.

But when the foundation is solid and sure, you can take the blows, stand strong, recover, and live with joy and hope. Only one foundation is sure and foolproof: Jesus Christ. Everything else you build upon will fail you.

The three things that helped me get through those times were my faith, my family and my friends.

-- Rick Hendrick

In the building of your life, you must start with a foundation in Jesus Christ, or the first trouble that shows up will knock you down.

CLOTHES HORSE

Read Genesis 37:1-11.

"Israel loved Joseph more than all his children, because he was the son of his old age: and he made him a coat of many colours" (v. 3) (KJV).

Benny Parsons once blamed a hideous racing uniform for his losing a race.

In 1965 he showed up at Daytona to race and discovered he needed a flameproof uniform to drive. His only driving experience was on small dirt tracks near Detroit, so he had no idea what a flameproof uniform even looked like. He saw at the track that officials had "a huge kettle, like when your grandmother boiled clothing" in which they boiled water and "put this chemical in there that rendered clothing flameproof."

His only uniform consisted of a T-shirt and a pair of white pants, so Parsons sent a crew member to a department store to buy a pair of white coveralls. The "uniform" was about six sizes too large, but it was okay. "It was all the guy could find. I had to roll the sleeves up. It was kind of baggy. We put it in the kettle, it rendered it flameproof and that was my uniform," Parsons said.

That "uniform" looked a whole lot worse for the wear, though, after it came out of that kettle. The white coveralls came out a putrid brown color that looked like -- well, use your imagination. Parsons didn't care what he looked like; all that mattered was that he was running at Daytona.

NASCAR

He thought he had won the race and was trying to find Victory Lane when an official informed him he had been a lap down and hadn't won anything. He had pitted too soon on a caution and been lapped, the official explained. "I had never made a pit stop in my life, so maybe I did pit too soon," Parsons said. "But I always thought my uniform had something to do with it. It looked terrible. No way they wanted someone wearing something like that getting his picture taken in Victory Lane."

Contemporary society proclaims that it's all about the clothes. Buy that new suit or dress, those new shoes, and all the sparkling accessories, and you'll be a new person. The changes are only cosmetic, though; under those clothes, you're the same person. Consider Joseph, for instance, prancing about in his pretty new clothes; he was still a spoiled tattletale.

Jesus never taught that we should run around half-naked or wear only second-hand clothes from the local mission. He did warn us, though, against making consumer items such as clothes a priority in our lives. A follower of Christ seeks to emulate Jesus not through material, superficial means such as wearing special clothing like a robe and sandals. Rather, the disciple desires to match Jesus' inner beauty and serenity -- whether the clothes the Christian wears are the sables of a king or the rags of a pauper.

Jeff Gordon came in wearing Nikes while everyone else was wearing cowboy boots.

-- Team owner Ray Evernham

**Where Jesus is concerned,
clothes don't make the person; faith does.**

PLAN AHEAD

Read Psalm 33:1-15.

"The plans of the Lord stand firm forever, the purposes of his heart through all generations" (v. 11).

The plan Ned Jarrett came up with to enter NASCAR has been described as the most "harebrained scheme" ever. But it worked.

Jarrett won the NASCAR Sportsmanship championship in 1957 and '58, but he still couldn't convince a top car owner to give him a chance with a stock car. He had to get creative, and in 1959, he got his chance when Junior Johnson decided he was going to build a new Dodge and sell the Ford he had driven for a year or so for $2,000.

Jarrett figured that Ford was exactly the car he needed to establish his reputation in the Grand Nationals. The problem was that he didn't have nearly that much money. That's when he got creative; that's when he came up with his "harebrained" plan.

Two Grand National events were slated for Myrtle Beach and Charlotte on successive weekend nights. They each paid $800 to win with a $100 appearance fee. "I quickly figured how I could work this thing out," Jarrett said. He wrote a check for the car on Friday after the banks closed, figuring he would cover the check by winning both races and kicking in $200 of his own.

He won at Myrtle Beach, but cut his hands so badly he could barely grip the wheel. He had no choice but to enter at Charlotte, but his injury forced him out of the car early. His harebrained scheme appeared done for, but Joe Weatherly saw the problem and took over. After blowing an engine, Junior Johnson hopped into Jarrett's car and brought the Ford home to victory. Neither Weatherly nor Johnson would accept any money from Jarrett. Monday morning the check cleared the bank. Jarrett had his car and was on his way.

Successful living takes planning. You go to school to improve your chances for a better paying job. You use blueprints to build your home. You plan for retirement. You map out your vacation to have the best time. You even plan your children -- sometimes.

Your best-laid plans, however, sometimes get wrecked by events and circumstances beyond your control. The economy goes into the tank; a debilitating illness strikes; a hurricane hits. Life is capricious and thus no plans -- not even your best ones -- are foolproof.

But you don't have to go it alone. God has plans for your life that guarantee success as God defines it if you will make him your planning partner. God's plan for your life includes joy, love, peace, kindness, gentleness, and faithfulness, all the elements necessary for truly successful living for today and for all eternity. And God's plan will not fail.

We don't want to go out there and wreck cars to get on TV, that's never the plan.
-- Michael McDowell after his 2008 crash was repeatedly shown on television

Your plans may ensure a successful life; God's plans will ensure a successful eternity.

GOOD SPORTS

Read Titus 2:1-8.

"Show integrity, seriousness and soundness of speech that cannot be condemned, so that those who oppose you may be ashamed because they have nothing bad to say about us" (vv. 7b, 8).

T here was cheating going on from day one."

So declared Hill Overton, Jr., who spent fifty years as a broadcaster and track announcer, about NASCAR. Sportsmanship has also been going on from day one.

On June 19, 1949, in Charlotte, what became known as the Cup Series was born -- and cheating was involved in the outcome. Glenn Dunnaway led the 33-car field to the finish line in a 1947 Ford. In the post-race inspection, though, Bill France discovered that Dunnaway's rear springs had been altered with a wedge. In a practice common among whiskey-running cars to add speed, Dunnaway's Ford had a wooden block inserted to jack up the springs on one side.

France immediately disqualified Dunnaway and declared Jim Roper and his Lincoln the winner. Roper had driven from Kansas after reading about the race in *Smilin' Jack,* a popular comic strip drawn by a racing enthusiast.

So much for the cheating. In what was described as "a display of sportsmanship and generosity that would come to define the sport," the drivers felt sorry for Dunnaway, who had not known his car had been illegally altered. So they passed the hat, and Dunnaway wound up with more money than he would have received had he kept his victory. His rather hacked off car owner got nothing.

Such is the way it is with NASCAR drivers and car owners. They "cheat to gain an advantage one minute, then show compassion and camaraderie the next if one of their competitors needed a hand."

One of life's paradoxes is that many who would never consider cheating on the tennis court or the racquetball court to gain an advantage think nothing of doing so in other areas of their life. In other words, the good sportsmanship they practice on the golf course or the Monopoly board doesn't carry over. They play with the truth, cut corners, abuse others verbally, run roughshod over the weaker, and generally cheat whenever they can to gain an advantage on the job or in their personal relationships.

But good sportsmanship is a way of living, not just of playing. Shouldn't you accept defeat without complaint (You don't have to like it.); win gracefully without gloating; treat your competition with fairness, courtesy, generosity, and respect? That's the way one team treats another in the name of sportsmanship.

That's the way one person treats another in the name of Jesus.

If you ain't cheating, you ain't trying.

-- NASCAR expression

Sportsmanship -- treating others with courtesy, fairness, and respect -- is a way of living, not just a way of playing.

THE FUNERAL

Read Romans 6:3-11.

"If we died with Christ, we believe that we will also live with him" (v. 8).

Dale Earnhardt's funeral, interestingly enough, wasn't about Dale Earnhardt the racing legend at all, but rather about something much more important: Dale Earnhardt the man.

The ceremony on Feb. 22, 2001, was held in Calvary Church in Charlotte. The only reminder that this was not the funeral of an ordinary mortal was a red, white, and black floral arrangement in the shape of Earnhardt's "3." Nothing else connected the service to The Intimidator's storied career. Two ministers spoke briefly, and longtime friend Randy Owens of the band Alabama sang and played his acoustic guitar. The cavernous church wasn't even full because attendance was limited to invited guests, though the service was televised nationally.

But who was present and what they said revealed that this was not an everyday funeral for an everyday man. "None of us were ready to let Dale go," Rusty Wallace said of his friend and rival. "God only created one Dale Earnhardt and no one will ever replace him." Junior Johnson said NASCAR "will get by, but it's going to hurt. It's a sad day for NASCAR and the sport." President George W. Bush sent an aide to the funeral along with personal expressions of his sadness and sympathy.

Earnhardt's widow, Teresa, spoke the only words for the family.

NASCAR

At the funeral's conclusion, she walked to the front of the church and blew two kisses toward the crowd. She whispered "Thank you, thank you" before leading her daughter, Taylor, out. After only 22 minutes, it was over.

Chances are you won't get the kind of funeral that merits national television, the kind of send-off usually reserved for the likes of kings, popes, presidents -- and Dale Earnhardt. Still, you want a good funeral. You want a decent crowd, you want folks to shed some tears, and you want some reasonably distinguished-looking types to stand behind a lectern and say some very nice things about you. Especially if they're all true.

But have you ever been to a funeral where the deceased you knew and the deceased folks were talking about were two different people? Where everyone struggled to say something nice about the not-so-dearly departed? Or a funeral that was little more than an empty acknowledgement that death is the end of all hope. Sad, isn't it?

Exactly what does make a good funeral, one where people laugh, love, and remember warmly and sincerely amid their tears? Jesus does. His presence transforms a mourning of death into a celebration of life.

It was a simple, solemn, brief memorial, and when it was over, everybody went racin'.
-- *CBS News on Dale Earnhardt's funeral*

Amid tears there is hope; amid death
there is resurrection – if Jesus is at the funeral.

MUDSLINGING

Read Isaiah 1:15-20.

"Though your sins are like scarlet, they shall be as white as snow; though they are red as crimson, they shall be like wool" (v. 18).

Buddy Baker once took a ride on a stretcher after a crash and wound up facedown in the mud.

In 1967, Baker was leading the race at a track in Maryville, TN, when he "felt this little rumble." When he went into a turn, his tire blew, and his car crashed headfirst into a wall. Baker was dazed, maybe unconscious for a moment, and had broken ribs.

An ambulance dutifully and promptly responded, and that's when Baker's real trouble began. The duo from the ambulance, whom Baker called "Bubba and Barney Fife," first tried to pull him headfirst out of his car without unhooking his safety harness.

When they finally got Baker loaded onto a stretcher and into the ambulance, they sped off without locking down the stretcher's wheels or securing the back door. To Baker's horror, as soon as the ambulance headed up the high-banked track for the hospital, the stretcher rolled into the door and the door opened, dumping the stretcher -- and Baker -- onto the track. The race was under caution; the cars were still running. "I got one arm out and started waving my hand at them a little," Baker said.

The drivers managed to dodge the stretcher, but Baker kept on rolling until he left the pavement. The gurney's wheels then hit mud and dug in, unceremoniously flipping Baker -- who was still strapped to the stretcher -- face first into the mud. When "Bubba and Barney" came running up and frantically wanted to know if we were OK, Baker told them, "If I ever get off this thing, I'm going to kill you."

You've probably never pullled a Buddy Baker and taken a ride on a stretcher and wound up facedown in the mud. You may not be a fan of mud boggin'. Still, you've worked on your car, planted a garden, played touch football in the rain, or endured some military training. You've been dirty.

Dirt, grime, and mud aren't the only sources of stains, however. We can also get dirty spiritually by not living in accordance with God's commands, by doing what's wrong, or by not doing what's right. We all experience temporary shortcomings and failures; we all slip and fall into the mud.

Whether we stay there or not, though, is a function of our relationship with Jesus. For the followers of Jesus, sin is not a way of life; it's an abnormality, so we don't stay in the filth. We seek a spiritual bath by expressing regret and asking for God's pardon in Jesus' name. God responds by washing our soul white as snow with his forgiveness.

It was the dustiest place I've ever seen. When the race started, it looked like someone had dropped a bomb.
                        -- Track owner Clay Earles on the first stock car race
                                      at Martinsville Speedway

When your soul gets dirty, a powerful and
thorough cleansing agent is available
for the asking: God's forgiveness.

DOWNRIGHT CRAZY

Read Luke 13:31-35.

"Some Pharisees came to Jesus and said to him, 'Leave this place and go somewhere else. Herod wants to kill you.' He replied, 'Go tell that fox . . . I must keep going today and tomorrow and the next day'" (vv. 31-33).

David Pearson was reluctant to "go racing Grand National" as he put it because he was convinced the drivers were crazy.

Pearson started driving when he was ten and quit school in the tenth grade to get a job and buy a car. After deciding work in the local cotton mill wasn't for him, Pearson went to work in his brother's body shop.

He always wanted to race, though, "because I had always been crazy about cars." When he was fifteen, he decided to build himself a car to race. "I didn't know what to do with it," he recalled, but that didn't stop him. "I wasn't a mechanic, but I did all the work myself." He put the car together and started racing on quarter-mile tracks. The experience was everything Pearson expected: "It was a lot of fun."

So he began to race in the Spartanburg area, running the little dirt tracks, winning a lot of races, making more money than he had in the cotton mill, and working on his car under a tree or in back of the house. Folks began to suggest he run at Darlington -- but Pearson wasn't interested. "They'd talk about Darlington and rubbing the guardrail, running 130 miles an hour, and I'd think,

Them guys are crazy. Man, I wouldn't do that."

But a friend forced his hand by starting a local David Pearson fan club and raising the money for him to buy a car and get into Grand National racing in 1960. By the time the reluctant racer retired in 1986, he had won 105 races, second only to Richard Petty, and was a three-time champion. Apparently, David Pearson was very good at being crazy.

What some see as crazy often is shrewd instead. Like the time you went into business for yourself or when you decided to go back to school. Maybe it was when you fixed up that old house. Or when you bought that new company's stock.

You know a good thing when you see it but are also shrewd enough to spot something that's downright crazy. Jesus was that way too. He knew that entering Jerusalem was in complete defiance of all apparent reason and logic since a whole bunch of folks who wanted to kill him were waiting for him there.

Nevertheless, he went because he also knew that when the great drama had played out he would defeat not only his personal enemies but the most fearsome enemy of all: death itself.

It was, after all, a shrewd move that provided the way to your salvation.

Racing cars is not the safest thing. Maybe at times it's not the sanest thing.

-- *Michael Waltrip*

**It's so good it sounds crazy -- but it's not:
through faith in Jesus Christ,
you can have eternal life with God.**

STAR POWER

Read Luke 10:1-3, 17-20.

"The Lord appointed seventy-two others and sent them two by two ahead of him to every town and place where he was about to go" (v. 1).

Many of today's drivers are superstars, often on television and the covers of magazines, their faces on all sorts of products, their names well known. It wasn't like that, though, in the 1960s until one man emerged as NASCAR's first real star. He was Glenn "Fireball" Roberts.

His No. 22 Pontiac "became the most famous car in the land," and he was the nation's most famous driver. "Everybody in the South and those around the county who followed stock car racing knew the name Fireball Roberts." Bob Latford, who worked PR at Charlotte Motor Speedway during Roberts' heyday, called him "the first superstar."

Roberts was inducted into the International Motorsports Hall of Fame in 1990 and was named one of NASCAR's 50 Greatest Drivers in 1998. In a career that began in 1947 when he was 18 and ended with his death in 1964 when he was 35, Roberts won 33 times, including the 1962 Daytona 500.

Latford described him as "a smart driver," one of the first who "drove with his head as much as with his foot. A lot of the early pioneers were just flat-out drivers." But Roberts "realized where the money was and how to take care of the equipment."

NASCAR

What separated Roberts from the pack was more than his driving ability. "He was a big guy, athletic-looking, and he could speak well, which made him an excellent representative," Latford recalled. He became the sports' spokesman, frequently appearing on television, a rare event for drivers of that era. He was a star.

A racing team is like other organizations in that it may have a star in the driver, but the star would be nothing without the supporting cast. It's the same in a private company, in a government bureaucracy, in a military unit, and just about any other team of people with a common goal.

That includes the team known as a church. It may have its "star" in the preacher, who is – like the driver, the quarterback, or the company CEO – the most visible representative of the team. Preachers are, after all, God's paid, trained professionals.

But when Jesus assembled a team of seventy-two folks, he didn't have anybody on the payroll or any seminary graduates. All he had were no-names who loved him. And nothing has changed. God's church still depends on those whose only pay is the satisfaction of serving and whose only qualification is their love for God.

God's church needs you.

Fireball Roberts was perhaps the most nearly perfect of all stock-car drivers.

-- Charlotte News *writer Max Muhleman*

Yes, the church needs its professional clergy, but it also needs those who serve as volunteers because they love God; the church needs you.

FAMILY AFFAIR

Read Mark 3:31-35.

*"[Jesus] said, 'Here are my mother and my brothers!
Whoever does God's will is my brother and sister and
mother'" (vv. 34-35).*

Ryan Newman's win at Daytona in 2008 was a family affair.

That he was even in the field of the fiftieth running of the Daytona 500 was a family affair. Newman comes from what has been described as "a blue-collar, tight-knit, hard-working family." His parents scrimped to put him through Purdue University and then managed to come up with some extra cash to help Newman pursue his dream of racing. His family, especially his wife, Krissie, stood by him and kept the faith even while he endured a horrendous streak of 81 races without a win dating back to 2005 -- broken by the Daytona triumph.

Newman uttered the requisite thanks during the victory celebration, especially for crew chief Roy McCauley, and his wife, Amy, who was battling cancer. He kept coming back, though, to one subject: family. He "couldn't stop talking about his father, who serves as his spotter, who was sobbing on the final lap over the radio as his son streaked across the finish line." When he was in victory lane, Newman said his dad "just told me he loved me, was proud of me and I gave (the love) right back to him. He was extremely emotional. We gave each other a big hug."

Newman also praised his mother, who was back home in

Indiana supporting a neighbor whose husband had died. He joked he had to end their phone conversation because "she was an absolute mess. She was bawling" and he "couldn't understand a word she was saying." With him to celebrate, too, were Krissie and his grandparents, "beaming with pride in the stands."

Newman's win didn't belong just to him, but to the whole family. Winning the world's biggest race was how he repaid his family for their love and their support.

Some wit said families are like fudge, mostly sweet with a few nuts. You can probably call the names of your sweetest relatives, whom you cherish, and of the nutty ones too, whom you mostly try to avoid at a family reunion.

Like it or not, you have a family, and that's God's doing. God cherishes the family so much that he chose to live in one as a son, a brother, and a cousin.

One of Jesus' more unsettling pronouncements was to redefine the family. No longer is it a single household of blood relatives or even a clan or a tribe. Jesus' family is the result not of an accident of birth but rather a conscious choice. All those who do God's will are members of Jesus' family.

What a startling and wonderful thought! You have family members out there you don't even know who stand ready to love you just because you're part of God's family.

I always wished I could race with my dad.

-- *Dale Earnhardt*

**For followers of Jesus, family comes
not from a shared ancestry but from a shared faith.**

THE GRUDGE

Read Matthew 6:7-15.

"If you forgive men when they sin against you, your heavenly Father will also forgive you. But if you do not forgive men their sins, your Father will not forgive your sins" (vv. 14-15).

If ever there were a grudge that you figure could never be patched up, it was that between NASCAR founder Bill France, Sr. and driver Curtis Turner.

In the early 1960s, Turner had the vision for Charlotte Motor Speedway. When his contractors hit granite, though, enormous cost overruns drove Turner to desperation. He cut a deal with the Teamsters Union, led by mobster Jimmy Hoffa. In exchange for an $800,000 loan, Turner promised to organize the NASCAR drivers into a union. Turner would also persuade NASCAR to allow pari-mutuel betting on the races.

He almost pulled it off as he signed up many of the drivers, including Fireball Roberts, Buck Baker, and Richard Petty. But then France called a meeting of the drivers, showed up with a pistol, and told the drivers he would "close every track I've got if you stay with this union deal." All the drivers except Turner and Tim Flock stayed with France and NASCAR. Without the union, the loan fell through, the union reps disappeared, and Turner lost everything he had.

Turner's wife, Bunny, called France and Turner "tight, good

friends." Turner, she said, was "like a brother" to France and admitted that the union effort "hurt Bill [France] so bad. Curtis had been so close to him. Curtis did what he had to do, and Bill did what he had to do." What France did was ban Turner and Flock from NASCAR for life. Their break was complete.

Or so it seemed. Before Curtis' death on Oct. 4, 1970, in a plane crash, the two men put their grudge behind them. France reinstated Turner and was a pallbearer at Turner's funeral. Their friendship ultimately triumphed.

It's probably pretty easy for you to recall times when somebody did you wrong. Have you held insistently onto your grudges so that the memory of each injury still drives up your blood pressure? Or have you forgiven that other person for what he or she did to you and shrugged it off as a lesson learned?

Jesus said to forgive others, which is exactly the sort of thing he would say. Extending forgiveness, though, is monumentally easier said than done. But here's the interesting part: You are to forgive for your sake, not for the one who injured you. When you forgive, the damage is over and done with. You can move on with your life, leaving the pain behind. The past – and that person -- no longer has power over you.

Holding a grudge is a way to self-destruction. Forgiving and forgetting is a way of life – a godly life.

Curtis and Bill patched it up before Curtis's death.
-- Bunny Turner Hall

**Forgiving others frees you from your past,
turning you loose to get on with your life.**

TEN TO REMEMBER

Read Exodus 20:1-17.

*"God spoke all these words: 'I am the Lord your God . . . .
You shall have no other gods before me'" (vv. 1, 3).*

In 1967, Richard Petty had the greatest season in the history of NASCAR. The King won 27 of his 48 starts, including an incredible ten in a row. In all, he was in the top five 38 times, dominance that has never been equaled.

In January 2008, ESPN's Mark Ashenfelter amused himself during the off-season by compiling his list of the Top 10 NASCAR Seasons with Petty in 1967 at the top. "We ran 48 races that year," Petty recalled, "so the team was constantly on the road, working on the car -- we mainly used only one. . . . There for a while, it seemed like we were simply rollin' from one Victory Lane into another one."

Petty's streak ended on Oct. 15 at Charlotte when he was swept into a wreck not of his own making. Buddy Baker won that race. Bobby Allison won the season's last two races.

Here's the rest of Ashenfelter's list of the ten best seasons in NASCAR history:

2) Jeff Gordon in 1998 with 13 wins and 26 top fives; 3) David Pearson's 1976 season with 10 wins in only 22 starts; 4) the 1981 season of Darrell Waltrip, which featured twelve wins and the first of two straight championships; 5) Dale Earnhardt's 1987 run as he led for more than one-third of the laps he completed; 6)

Cale Yarborough in 1978 when he won ten races and his third straight championship; 7) Jimmie Johnson's 2007 season, which featured ten wins, including four in a row; 8) Tim Flock in 1955, who won the championship and led a staggering 3,495 of the 6,208 laps he completed; 9) Bill Elliott's 1985 season in which he had 11 wins; and 10) Bobby Isaac in 1969 when he won 17 times despite completing only 31 races.

These are indeed ten seasons for NASCAR fans to remember.

You've got your list and you're ready to go: a gallon of paint and a water hose from the hardware store; chips, peanuts, and sodas from the grocery store for watching tonight's football game with your buddies; the tickets for the band concert. Your list helps you remember.

God also made a list once of things he wanted you to remember; it's called the Ten Commandments. Just as your list reminds you to do something, so does God's list remind you of how you are to act in your dealings with other people and with him. A life dedicated to Jesus is a life devoted to relationships, and God's list emphasizes that the social life and the spiritual life of the faithful cannot be sundered. God's relationship to you is one of unceasing, unqualified love, and you are to mirror that divine love in your relationships with others. In case you forget, you have a list.

If everyone would just live by the Bible and the Ten Commandments, see how much better the world would be.

-- Morgan Shepherd

God's list is a set of instructions on how you are to conduct yourself with other people and with him.

BAD IDEA

Read Mark 14:43-50.

*"The betrayer had arranged a signal with them: 'The one
I kiss is the man; arrest him and lead him away under
guard'" (v. 44).*

Harold Brasington didn't want to disturb his minnows, which
at first turned out to be a very bad idea but subsequently changed
racing history.

Ten years before Bill France built Daytona, Brasington built the
Darlington track, the first superspeedway, for Indy cars. He saw
the Indianapolis 500, was inspired, and realized he owned land
suitable for a track. He would build it and they would come.

On part of his land, Brasington already had a minnow farm,
and he didn't want to disturb his minnows. The track, therefore,
didn't wind up symmetrical as turn four was tighter than the
other turns to avoid the minnow farm.

Bad idea.

Indy car drivers quickly discovered they couldn't race on the
track because they consistently lost control of their cars on the
tight turn at the minnow farm. Its layout rendered the track unfit
for Indy car racing. With all his money invested, Brasington was
desperate. He scheduled some motorcycle races, but in practice
a few bikers met the tight turn and wound up with broken legs.
The races were cancelled.

Thus, because of his minnow farm, Brasington "was stuck

with a racetrack he didn't know what to do with" and that nobody wanted. But he finally did have a good idea. He called up France and asked for help in promoting a stock car race at Darlington. They struck a deal, and on Sept. 4, 1950, the first Southern 500 race was held at Darlington Speedway -- next to the minnow farm.

That sure-fire investment you made from a pal's hot stock tip. The expensive exercise machine that now traps dust bunnies under your bed. Blond hair. Telling your wife you wanted to eat at the restaurant with the waitresses in little shorts. They seemed like pretty good ideas at the time; they weren't.

We all have bad ideas in our lifetime. They provide some of our most crucial learning experiences. If Harold Brasington hadn't built a track with a bad layout, we may never have had stock-car racing at Darlington.

Some ideas, though, are so irreparably and inherently bad that we cannot help but wonder why they were even conceived in the first place. Almost two thousand years ago a man had just such an idea. Judas' betrayal of Jesus remains to this day one of the most heinous acts of treachery in history.

Turning his back on Jesus was a bad idea for Judas then; it's a bad idea for us now.

I knew in my head this morning we shouldn't have run it and we all decided as a group to do it, and I was one of the guys that decided to go ahead and run it so we should have known better than that.
-- Matt Kenseth after suffering engine failure

We all have some pretty bad ideas
during our lifetimes, but nothing
equals the folly of turning away from Jesus.

NASCAR

DAY 73

HOMESICK

Read 2 Corinthians 5:1-10.

*"We . . . would prefer to be away from the body and at
home with the Lord" (v. 8).*

In 2004, Tony Stewart did something that transformed his race
team and put him on track to win his second Cup title. He went
home to his free chocolate milk shakes.

The last race of the 2004 season was barely over when Stewart
announced he was moving back to Columbus, Ind., where he grew
up, after six years of living north of Charlotte. He had developed
the reputation as "NASCAR's stormiest driver," according to Lars
Anderson, but the move changed everything for his team -- and
that included Stewart.

"I'm just so much more relaxed now," he said. "Life isn't complicated for me here. And nobody really bothers me. My neighbors
think of me as the same punk kid who smacked baseballs into
their aluminum siding. . . . Where I need to be for my own peace
of mind is here."

Team member Ronny Crooks agreed that the move was good
for everyone. "Tony moving home has meant everything to our
team," he said. "Instead of looking at problems, Tony now looks
at solutions."

Maybe it has something to do with those free milk shakes. Bob
Franke owns the Columbus Dairy Queen, and he was the first
person to sponsor the young daredevil with a go-kart, big dreams,

NASCAR

and a heavy foot. "I gave him about $1,500 and all the shakes he could drink," Franke said. "I guess I should have signed him to a lifetime contract."

The move had an immediate effect on Stewart's career. In 2005, he won his second NEXTEL Cup Championship, joining Jeff Gordon as the only active, full-time driver to own multiple championships. (Jimmie Johnson subsequently joined them.)

So now Stewart is back home -- with his sister, those free shakes, and his neighbors and friends.

Home is not necessarily a matter of geography. It may be that place you share with your spouse and your children, whether it's Indiana or North Carolina. You may feel at home when you return to Daytona Beach, wondering why you were so eager to leave in the first place. Maybe the home you grew up in still feels like an old shoe, a little worn but comfortable and inviting.

God planted that sense of home in us because he is a God of place, and our place is with him. Thus, we may live a few blocks away from our parents and grandparents or we may relocate every few years, but we will still sometimes feel as though we don't really belong no matter where we are. We don't; our true home is with God in the place Jesus has gone ahead to prepare for us. We are homebodies and we are perpetually homesick.

I always knew you'd come back to Columbus. This is where you belong. And we'll always give you shakes.
-- Noel Franke to Tony Stewart

We are continually homesick for our real home, which is with God in Heaven.

NASCAR

DAY 74

THE ANSWER

Read Colossians 2:2-10.

*"My purpose is that they . . . may know the mystery of
God, namely, Christ, in whom are hidden all the treasures
of wisdom and knowledge" (vv. 2, 3).*

Start it up, drive it over to the Grand Canyon, and jump out."
That was the answer Lou LaRosa came up with for the rather
pressing problem he was facing.

One of NASCAR's legendary car builders, LaRosa got his start
in the late 1960s with the DiGard racing team based in Daytona
Beach. In January 1974, he and mechanic David Ifft were assigned
to tow a car in an open trailer to Riverside, California, for a
race. Before they left, LaRosa asked the more experienced Ifft if
they should drain the engine, but Ifft noted they were going to
California with all its sunny weather, so there was no need to
take out the drain plugs. They didn't.

In Arizona, Ifft startled LaRosa by announcing, "Stop. The
bungee came off and you ran over it." From Brooklyn, LaRosa
knew a "bungee" as a tie-down strap, and he said, "I swear I
thought I had run over a Japanese kamikaze pilot."

When he got under the car, LaRosa saw water and called Ifft's
attention to it. "That's just condensation," the mechanic replied.
That wasn't it at all, however.

Even though the hoses had been off, the motor had frozen
during the drive through Louisiana, and the block had cracked.

To Ifft's slightly panicked, "What are we doing to do?" came LaRosa's very panicked suggestion that they drive the car into the Grand Canyon. Ultimately, Ifft had a better answer for their problem, and they spent the night in a shopping center parking lot changing the motor.

Experience is essentially the uncovering of answers to some of life's questions, both trivial and profound. You often discover to your dismay that as soon as you learn a few answers, the questions change. Your children get older, your health worsens, your financial situation changes, your favorite NASCAR driver retires -- all situations requiring answers to a completely new set of difficulties.

No answers, though, are more important than those you seek in your search for God and the meaning of life because they determine your fate for all eternity. Since a life of faith is a journey and not a destination, the questions do indeed change with your circumstances. The "why" or the "what" you ask God when you're a teenager is vastly different from the quandaries you ponder as an adult. No matter how you phrase the question, though, the answer inevitably centers on Jesus. And that answer never changes.

When you're a driver and you're struggling in the car, you're looking for God to come out of the sky and give you a magical answer.
-- Rusty Wallace

It doesn't matter what the question is;
if it has to do with the issues of life
-- temporal or eternal -- the answer lies in Jesus.

DAY 75

PEACEMONGERS

Read Hebrews 12:14-17.

"Make every effort to live in peace with all men and to be holy" (v. 14).

Sometimes if you're going to act as a peacemaker, it helps to have a two-by-four handy.

In 1961 at the Asheville-Weaverville Speedway, the Western North Carolina 500 was halted after 258 laps because the track had deteriorated to the point where it became too dangerous to race on it. During a red-flag period after a crash on lap 208, NASCAR executive manager Pat Purcell told the drivers the race would be halted in fifty laps. The number was not accidental; that would be enough laps to make the race official. Purcell left the drivers with an ominous blessing: "I hope you can make it."

Perhaps anticipating the outrage that would result from their decision, NASCAR officials took advantage of the 50-lap period to slip out of their uniforms and skulk from the track. Sure enough, when the fans learned that 258 laps were all they were going to get, they rioted. They sealed the escape route by dragging a truck across the infield's access road. Two infield denizens approached the mob to mediate a peace; one was heaved into a lake and the other was tossed over a fence.

The best efforts of sheriff's deputies and some Carolina highway patrolmen were to no avail. Finally, a crewman on Bud Moore's team, Maurice "Pop" Eargle, all 6'6", 285 pounds of him, decided it was time to put an end to this foolishness. For his trouble, he was poked in the stomach with a two-by-four by one of the mob's leaders. Eargle promptly ripped the board away and whacked the guy beside the head. That took the steam out of the rioters, the crowd broke up, and the teams made their getaways without any further incidents.

Incidentally, Junior Johnson led all 258 laps and was declared the winner.

Perhaps you've never been in a brawl or a public brouhaha to match that of Pop Eargle and the rest of the crew. But maybe you retaliated when you got one elbow too many in a pickup basketball game. Or maybe you and your spouse or your teenager get into it occasionally, shouting and saying cruel things. Or road rage may be a part of your life.

While we do seem to live in a more belligerent, confrontational society than ever before, fighting is still not the solution to a problem. Rather, it only escalates the whole confrontation, leaving wounded pride, intransigence, and simmering hatred in its wake. Actively seeking and making peace is the way to a solution that lasts and heals broken relationships and aching hearts.

Peacemaking is not as easy as fighting, but it is much more courageous and a lot less painful. It is also the Jesus thing to do.

I got out and he went to beating on my fist with his nose.
-- *Bobby Allison on the infamous fight with Cale Yarborough at the 1979 Daytona 500*

Making peace instead of fighting takes courage and strength; it's also what Jesus would do.

DAY 76

THE PIONEER SPIRIT

Read Luke 5:1-11.

"So they pulled their boats up on shore, left everything and followed him" (v. 11).

Louise Smith is one of racing's true pioneers.

Smith lived in South Carolina when Bill France came to Greenville in the mid-1940s to promote a race. Admission was only a quarter, but attendance was still sparse at the races. France told the promoters they needed a woman driver to put folks in the grandstands and attract the media. They said they knew of only one woman who perhaps could handle it, one they called "a menace on the local roads." They told France, "She can drive, but we don't know whether she can drive on the track or not."

The woman was Louise Smith. The promoters contacted her, and Smith drove in the first race she ever saw. Officials told her, "If you see a red flag, stop." She saw a bunch of flags, including checkered and green ones, but no red flag, so after the race was over, she kept driving until officials put out the red flag to stop her. She finished third.

France asked her to come down to Daytona, and Smith went on to drive at Daytona's beach-and-road track from 1946 through 1952. The first time she entered, she kept it a secret from her husband. In 1947, she drove the family car on the highway down to Daytona and was subsequently involved in a seven-car pileup. "I tore that car up," she said. Nor surprisingly, her husband was a mite upset about the car, but he supported her racing after that. In 1949, she bought a Nash Ambassador and raced in some of NASCAR's first official events. Sara Christian and Ethel Mobley, Tim Flock's sister, joined her on the tracks in 1948, but Smith, who was elected in 1999 into the International Motorsports Hall of Fame, was NASCAR's first woman driver, a true trailblazer.

Going to a place in your life you've never been before requires a willingness to take risks and face uncertainty head-on. You may have never been present at the beginning of a new national sport, but you've had your moments when your latent pioneer spirit manifested itself. That time you changed careers, ran a marathon, volunteered at a homeless shelter, learned Spanish, or went back to school.

While attempting new things invariably begets apprehension, the truth is that when life becomes too comfortable and too familiar, it gets boring. The same is true of God, who is downright dangerous because he calls us to be anything but comfortable as we serve him. He summons us to continuously blaze new trails in our faith life, to follow him no matter what. Stepping out on faith is risky all right, but the reward is a life of accomplishment, adventure, and joy that cannot be equaled anywhere else.

I was just born to be wild. From the moment I hit the racetrack, it was exactly what I wanted.

-- *Louise Smith*

Unsafe and downright dangerous, God calls us
out of the place where we are comfortable
to a life of adventure and trailblazing in his name.

NOT WHAT THEY SEEM

Read Habakkuk 1:2-11.

"Why do you make me look at injustice? Why do you tolerate wrong? Destruction and violence are before me; there is strife, and conflict abounds" (v. 3).

A photograph taken of the finish of the first-ever Daytona 500 in 1959 generated such a buzz that it helped usher NASCAR into an era of unprecedented popularity -- but the photo wasn't what it seemed.

Taken by a fan and not a professional photographer, the shot has been described as "one of the iconic images in NASCAR history: a three-wide finish in the first major race at the newest and biggest track in the sport's signature event." The photograph of "three cars screaming to the finish line, side by side" created a buzz for stock-car racing and its brand new showplace. Richmond radio host Joe Kelly observed, "People a lot of times don't read, but a picture's worth a thousand words."

Kelly said that picture showed "three cars at a track with 42,000 people in a city that only had 37,000 people in it at the time. It propelled a lot of people to start thinking about NASCAR." The sensational photo also helped spread the word that the winner took home $19,000, which, as Kelly pointed out, "was a ton of money in those days."

The drivers in the famous photograph were Lee Petty, Johnny Beauchamp, and Joe Weatherly. The finish was so close that in

NASCAR

a day long before instant replay, NASCAR officials needed two days to declare Petty the winner over Beauchamp. Both men were convinced they had won.

And the third car that was nose-to-nose with Petty and Beauchamp and that was so vital in capturing the thrill and excitement of NASCAR for the world to see? Weatherly was a lap down and finished fifth. He wasn't competing for the win at all.

Sometimes in NASCAR things just aren't what they seem.

Sometimes in life things aren't what they seem either. In our violent and convulsive times, we must confront the possibility of a new reality: that we are helpless in the face of anarchy; that injustice, destruction, and violence are pandemic in and symptomatic of our modern age. It seems that anarchy is winning, that the system of standards, values, and institutions we have cherished is crumbling while we watch.

But we should not be deceived or disheartened. God is in fact the arch-enemy of chaos, the creator of order and goodness and the architect of all of history. God is in control. We often misinterpret history as the record of mankind's accomplishments -- which it isn't -- rather than the unfolding of God's plan -- which it is. That plan has a clearly defined end: God will make everything right. In that day things will be what they seem.

That photograph right there propelled the sport into a new world.
-- Radio host Joe Kelly

**The forces of good and decency often seem
helpless before evil's power, but don't be fooled;
God is in control and will set things right.**

SURPRISE, SURPRISE

Read Judges 6:11-23.

"'But Lord,' Gideon asked, 'how can I save Israel? My clan is the weakest in Manasseh, and I am the least in my family'" (v. 15).

The most jaw-dropping surprise of Junior Johnson's life saved a struggling NASCAR and changed the face of the sport forever.

When Bill France announced in 1970 that he would require restrictor plates on cars at the superspeedways, Detroit's Big Three began to withdraw their sponsorship. NASCAR was at a critical juncture in its history as sponsorship money was shrinking while the costs of operating a team were skyrocketing.

Johnson had retired as a driver in 1966 but continued to operate as a car owner. Like everyone else at the time, he was feeling the economic pinch, but he had an idea. The big tobacco companies had recently been booted off television by the government as the antismoking campaign switched into high gear. Since R.J. Reynolds now had some advertising money left over, they might just be willing to use some of it to sponsor a racing team -- preferably Johnson's team.

Johnson secured an interview with a Reynolds executive who asked him how much sponsorship money he was looking for. Johnson swallowed and decided to go for it hard: About eight hundred thousand dollars to sponsor my team, he replied. Then came the surprise. The executive smiled and said, "We were thinking more along the lines of eight or nine hundred million dollars."

When Johnson picked himself up off the floor, he contacted France. Reynolds sponsored its first race, the Winston 500 at Talladega, in May 1971. NASCAR has never been the same.

Do what?

The night your wife announced she was pregnant. The day your boss said he wanted you to transfer to the branch office -- in another state. That afternoon your son declared he wanted to drop out of school. Surprise, surprise!

You know the look and the feel when you are suddenly surprised by a situation you neither sought nor were prepared for. You've had the wide-eyed look and the turmoil in your midsection when you were suddenly singled out and found yourself in a situation you neither sought nor were prepared for.

Like being called to serve God in some way. You may feel the same way Gideon did when God surprised him, quailing at the very notion of being audacious enough to teach Sunday school, lead a small group study, or coordinate a high school prayer club. After all, who's worthy enough to do anything like that?

The truth is that nobody is – but that doesn't seem to matter to God. And it's his opinion, not yours, that counts.

There's no bigger surprise than to be tooling along at 200 miles per hour and suddenly getting hit from the rear.

-- Darrell Waltrip

**God is just full of surprises,
including wanting you to serve him.**

MIDDLE OF NOWHERE

Read Genesis 28:10-22.

"When Jacob awoke from his sleep, he thought, 'Surely the Lord is in this place, and I was not aware of it'" (v. 16).

You can't get there from here, but there it was big as you please: a NASCAR Nextel Cup flag.

On May 24, 2007, the flag was planted truly in the middle of nowhere, or at least at the very top of it: the summit of Mt. Everest, 29,035 feet above sea level. The day was quite blustery -- 40 below zero with wind gusts of 40 miles an hour -- when NASCAR fan Patrick Hickey reached the top of the world.

As he climbed, Hickey kept a blog of his journey and wrote that "although he was capable of overcoming fatigue, frozen conditions and feelings of isolation, he was troubled by an absence of NASCAR news." A professor of nursing at the University of South Carolina, Hickey wondered about the outcome of the races and the fate of his favorite driver, Jeff Gordon. About five hundred folks from twenty different countries promptly responded with NASCAR updates and with money for the nursing scholarships Hickey was funding by raising $1 for every foot he climbed.

A fan contacted NASCAR officials, who asked Hickey to plant the flag on the summit. "My phone rings and someone asks where they can meet me to hand off the flag," Hickey said. "I told him I was in a tent, behind a boulder at base camp, at about 17,600 feet." The flag came via a medical helicopter that was rescuing two injured climbers. "A pilot walks up to me, asks if I'm Patrick Hickey and hands me an envelope with a United States postage stamp on it," Hickey said.

NASCAR's flag was on the last leg of its journey to the middle of nowhere.

Ever been to Level Cross, NC? Or Dawsonville, GA? Think you could find Cambridge, WI, or Richburg, SC, with its 300 or so residents? Get to St. Louis and maybe you can find Fenton. You may know that respectively they're the birthplaces of Richard Petty, Bill Elliott, Matt Kenseth, Buck Baker, and Rusty Wallace, but they're all small towns that dot the American countryside, places you have to intentionally search out to visit.

They seem to be in the middle of nowhere, just hamlets we zip through on our way to somewhere important.

But don't be misled; those villages are indeed special and wonderful. That's because God is in Unadilla, GA – birthplace of David Ragan – and Enumclaw, WA – birthplace of Kasey Kayne – just as he is in Las Vegas, birthplace of Kyle and Kurt Busch.

Even when you are far off the roads well traveled, you are with God. As Jacob discovered one rather astounding morning, the middle of nowhere is, in fact, holy ground -- because God is there.

The house is up there, but this is his home.
-- spoken of Junior Johnson's cinderblock building, which is away from
the house that is on a remote farm out from Hamptonville
in a corner of Yadkin county up the road from Winston-Salem, N.C.

**No matter how far off the beaten path you travel,
you are still on holy ground because God is there.**

OUT WITH THE OLD

Read Hebrews 8:3-13.

"The ministry Jesus has received is as superior to theirs as the covenant of which he is mediator is superior to the old one, and it is founded on better promises" (v. 6).

Judging by NASCAR's unprecedented popularity today, few fans or drivers would swap what they have for the way things were a generation ago. Larry Shankle is an exception.

Shankle was involved with stock car racing for more than two decades. He was a crew chief before he left the sport in the 1980s. For him, that period -- not today -- was NASCAR's golden age when "things were simpler, a far cry from the modern form we know today."

Teams ran more races with no fancy car haulers or luxury mobile homes. "We would drive to races across the country in a big Ford truck, and it didn't even have air conditioning," he remembered. The teams had no spacious garages to work in. They would stop in small towns and spread the word that they needed a place to work. Inevitably, a farmer would offer up a barn, and Shankle would transform it into a makeshift garage. "It was great back then; it was like a family." Those hospitable farm families would also usually invite the crews into their homes and to their dinner tables.

Shankle doesn't like the way the sport moved from smaller-market tracks like North Wilkesboro to larger markets in

NASCAR

Texas and California. "When they took the Southern 500 from Darlington, it was like taking a baby from its mama," Shankle said. "It was just wrong."

Larry Shankle would trade today's sport for the old days in a heartbeat.

Most of us like new stuff, though. Your car's running fine, but the miles are adding up. Time for a trade-in. Your TV set is still delivering a sharp picture, but those HDTV's are really something. Same with the newer, faster computers. And how about those lawn mowers that turn on a dime?

Out with the old, in with the new — we're always looking for the newest thing on the market. In our faith life, that means the new covenant God gave us through Jesus Christ. An old covenant did exist, one based on the law God handed down to the Hebrew people. But God used this old covenant as the basis to go one better and establish a covenant available to the whole world. This new way is a covenant of grace between God and anyone who lives a life of faith in Jesus.

Don't get caught waiting for a newer, improved covenant, though; the promises God gave us through Jesus couldn't get any better.

NASCAR has changed so much in the last five years because you don't have as many of the good old Southern boys as you used to.
-- J.J. Yeley

**No matter how old it is,
it just doesn't get any better
than God's new covenant through Jesus Christ.**

USING YOUR HEAD

Read Job 28.

"The fear of the Lord -- that is wisdom, and to shun evil is understanding" (v. 28).

T im Flock once suffered an injury that is rather bizarre even by NASCAR standards: A truck ran over his head.

Flock retired from racing in 1961 after a successful career that included thirty-nine wins and NASCAR driving championships in 1952 and 1955. He might well have won in 1953 except for his strange accident.

When Flock pulled into the infield in the afternoon for the July 4th race in Spartanburg, he had towed his Hudson all day and all night to get from a race in Ontario. Since the race wasn't to begin until 8 p.m., Flock decided to get some badly needed sleep, so he simply stretched out beside his car to take a nap.

As Flock found out later, a man was putting Champion spark plug decals all over the place, backing his pickup truck up as he went. As Flock put it, "He backed [the truck] about a hundred and fifty feet onto my dang head."

Flock woke up "when I heard the muffler, and before I could move, the left rear tire made a track across my head -- you can't holler with a car sitting on your chest -- and when the [truck] stopped, the tire was up on my head."

When the Champion man discovered what he had done, his reaction was not surprising. "When the driver looked down and

NASCAR

saw me, he was so scared he fell out of the car," Flock recalled. Some state troopers helped lift the truck off Flock, and he was hospitalized for a few days.

More than thirty-five years later, he ran into the "poor boy who ran over [me], and it still worries him about backing over my head."

You're a thinking person. When you talk about using your head, you're not speaking about employing it to chock a truck as Tim Flock did. Instead, you're speaking of thinking things through. Logic and reason are part of your psyche. A coach's bad call frustrates you and your children's inexplicable behavior flummoxes you. Why can't people just use the good sense God gave them?

That goes for matters of faith too. Jesus doesn't tell you to turn your brain off when you walk into a church or open the Bible. In fact, when you seek Jesus, you seek him heart, soul, body, and mind. The mind of the master should be the master of your mind so that you consider every situation in your life through the critical lens of the mind of Christ. With your head *and* your heart, you encounter God, who is, after all, the true source of wisdom.

To know Jesus is not to stop thinking; it is to start thinking divinely.

We just out thunk 'em there at the end.
    -- Richard Petty after winning his seventh Daytona 500 in 1981

**Since God is the source of all wisdom,
it's only logical that you encounter him
with your mind as well as your emotions.**

PLAYING WITH PAIN

Read 2 Corinthians 1:3-7.

"Just as the sufferings of Christ flow over into our lives, so also through Christ our comfort overflows" (v. 5).

Dale Earnhardt went through a slump in 1996, '97, and '98, not because his skills diminished, but because he was racing hurt.

Earnhardt was the points leader going into the DieHard 500 in July 1996 at Talledega. Late in the race, though, Ernie Irvan lost control of his #28 Ford Thunderbird, igniting a frightening crash that drove Earnhardt's #3 Chevrolet into the wall at almost 200 miles per hour. Earnhardt's car then flipped and slid across the track right into the path of the race traffic. His car was hit in the roof and in the windshield. (The long-term result was NASCAR's mandating of the "Earnhardt Bar," a metal brace that reinforced the roof.)

Earnhardt climbed out of his car, waved to the crowd, and refused to be loaded onto a stretcher. He was severely injured, however, suffering a broken collarbone, sternum, and shoulder blade. Many fans and observers expected that the injuries would end his season.

Earnhardt refused to let his injuries keep him off the track, though. The next week he started at Indianapolis before exiting the car at the first pit stop. The next weekend at Watkins Glen he qualified with the fastest time. But Earnhardt did not win again in 1996, and in 1997 he went winless for the second time in his career.

He appeared to be back on track when he won the Daytona 500 in 1998, his lone victory there, but the rest of the season went badly, and he finished eighth in the final point standings.

Crew chief Larry McReynolds diagnosed the problem: Earnhardt "was a bummed up individual, and he was hurting for a long time. He played hurt for a good two to three years." Only after Earnhardt had surgery between the 1999 and 2000 season to fix his neck did he return to form, no longer playing with pain.

Since you live on Earth and not in Heaven, you are forced to play with pain. Whether it's a car wreck that left you shattered, the end of a relationship that left you battered, or a loved one's death that left you tattered -- pain finds you and challenges you to keep going.

While God's word teaches that you will reap what you sow, life also teaches that pain and hardship are not necessarily the result of personal failure. Pain in fact can be one of the tools God uses to mold your character and change your life.

What are you to do when you are hit full-speed by the awful pain that seems to choke the very will to live out of you? Where is your consolation, your comfort, and your help? In almighty God, whose love will never fail.

When life knocks you to your knees, you're closer to God than ever before.

You hit the wall head-on; it hurts.

-- Joe Nemechek

When life hits you with pain, turn to God
for comfort, consolation, and hope.

TEAM PLAYERS

Read 1 Corinthians 12:4-13; 27-31.

"Now to each one the manifestation of the Spirit is given for the common good" (v. 7).

Far away from the fury, the frenzy, and the fame of race day, they are rarely seen or heard by the fan. Yet their contribution to the racing team is so valuable that Jerry Bonkowski once wrote that few champions in history could have done it without them.

They are the spotters, the guys with the best seats in the house except that they never sit down. They're on their feet from green flag to checkered flag, perched atop the grandstands, constantly watching and talking to their driver. The tools of their trade are a two-way radio and a set of binoculars. Beyond those practical items, though, they must have "a pair of eagle eyes and a knack for anticipating trouble on the race track." The job of the spotter is to keep his driver and his car out of trouble, letting them both finish the race in one piece.

Spotting for Reed Sorenson, Loren Ranier compared his job to "riding shotgun," always telling Sorenson "to watch out for this or for that." The priority for the spotter, Ranier said, "is to keep a driver safe." They have been compared to offensive linemen protecting their quarterbacks.

The spotters let the drivers know what's going on around them, in front of them, and behind them, who's coming up fast, what line is moving. They talk to other spotters, relaying messages and information. The relationship between driver and spotter requires absolute trust; they work as a team.

Spotting for Dario Franchitti, Mike Calinoff defined success for the spotter: "If we finish in the top 20 with all the fenders on and [the driver] is healthy and safe, it's a great day."

Most accomplishments are the result of teamwork, whether it's a college football team, the running of a household, the completion of a project at work, the winning of the Daytona 500, or a dance recital. Disparate talents and gifts work together for the common good and the greater goal.

A church works exactly the same way. At its most basic, a church is a team assembled by God. A shared faith drives the team members and impels them toward shared goals. As a successful racing team must include drivers, mechanics, spotters, and pit crews, so must a church be composed of people with different spiritual and personal gifts. The result is something greater than everyone involved.

What makes a church team different from others is that the individual efforts are expended for the glory of God and not self. The nature of a church member's particular talents doesn't matter; what does matter is that those talents are used as part of God's team.

Money may be the most important element in modern-day stock car racing, but team chemistry runs a very close second.

-- *Bill Elliott*

**A church is a team of people
using their various talents and gifts for God,
the source of all those abilities to begin with.**

DAY 84

HOW WE LEAVE

Read 2 Kings 2:1-12.

"A chariot of fire and horses of fire appeared and separated the two of them, and Elijah went up to heaven in a whirlwind" (v. 11).

Fireball Roberts carefully planned out how he would leave his racing career behind. It just didn't go the way he planned.

With thirty-three Grand National wins behind him, Roberts decided to retire after the 1964 season. He was all set to begin a new life and a new career. Articulate and comfortable in front of a television camera and doing public relations, he signed a contract with a beer company in December 1963 to be its spokesman. He anticipated doing some commentary for NASCAR.

His divorce was finalized on April 15, 1964, and Roberts and Judy Judge set a marriage date of June 6. As Judge put it, "Glenn was so smart, so talented and capable. I felt like he was just beginning to become the man he was meant to be. He loved what our future held for us and was excited about going into the commentary business."

The 1964 racing season progressed until Roberts had three races to run before his career was over: Charlotte, Daytona, and Darlington. On the eighth lap at Charlotte Motor Speedway on May 24, his car spun backwards and slammed into the edge of the concrete wall of the backstretch.

The car exploded into flames upon impact. Ned Jarrett left his car and pulled Roberts out as he screamed, "Ned, help me. I'm on fire." Roberts suffered burns on most of his body and was airlifted to Charlotte Memorial Hospital in "extremely critical" condition.

He fought valiantly to live while the racing world prayed, but suddenly on July 2 Glenn "Fireball" Roberts died as pneumonia and blood poisoning proved to be too much. "I just didn't think it was going to happen," Judge said.

Like Fireball Roberts and Elijah, we can't always choose the exact circumstances under which we leave.

You probably haven't always chosen the moves you've made in your life. Perhaps your company transferred you. A landlord didn't renew your lease. An elderly parent needed your care.

Sometimes the only choice we have about leaving is the manner in which we go, whether we depart with style and grace or not. Our exit from life is the same way. Unless we usurp God's authority over life and death, we can't choose how we die, just how we handle it. Perhaps the most frustrating aspect of dying is that we have at most very little control over the process. As with our birth, our death is in God's hands. We finally must surrender to his will even if we have spent a lifetime refusing to do so.

We do, however, control our destination. How we leave isn't up to us; where we spend eternity is -- and that depends on our relationship with Jesus.

In a race, what I fear most is fire.

-- Fireball Roberts

**How and when we go isn't up to us;
where we go is.**

DAY 85

MYSTERIOUS WAYS

Read Romans 11:25-36.

"O the depth of the riches and wisdom and knowledge of God! How unsearchable are his judgments and how inscrutable his ways!" (v. 33 NRSV)

A reporter showed up at Charlotte Motor Speedway one day in the 1970s to write a column -- but he tried to tackle a subject so complex and mysterious that he wound up totally befuddled and confused and never did get that column written.

Tom Higgins was in the speedway's press box when that newspaperman confidently sat down to write his story. It didn't go very well, Higgins recalled. The reporter wrote a paragraph, "then yelled 'You idiot! That's not it.'" He ripped the paper from the typewriter, violently wadded it up, and vehemently tossed it across the room. He inserted new paper and started again. And again. And again, each time insulting himself.

Finally, after ninety minutes during which he had succeeded only in littering the press box with 56 wadded pieces of paper, he screamed, "This story is impossible to write!" He then packed his typewriter up and left.

What was so difficult? The reporter had tried to write a story on Morris Metcalfe, NASCAR's chief scorer, and the scoring system he had devised. This was long before today's high-tech gadgetry that enables NASCAR officials to determine instantly the exact position of all cars anytime, and Metcalfe had devised a system that he worked virtually to perfection. He had a scoring corps of two persons per car. They logged each lap and the time and held up scoring cards, and Morris entered the information in his log.

But exactly how the system worked was largely a mystery -- especially to that reporter and his readers.

We often love a good mystery because we relish the challenge of uncovering what somebody else wants to hide. We are intrigued by a perplexing whodunit, a rousing round of Clue, or Perry Mason reruns.

Some mysteries, however, – perhaps like NASCAR's outdated scoring system -- are simply beyond our knowing. For instance, when we declare that the Good Lord sure works in mysterious ways, we are acknowledging that even though God has revealed much about himself, especially through Jesus, much about God remains mysterious. Why does he tolerate the existence of evil? What does he really look like? Why is he so fond of bugs?

We can't see the divine machinations. We can see only the results, appreciate that God was behind them all, and give him thanks and praise.

We can and do know for sure, though, that God is love, and so we live each day in trust, assured that one day all mysteries will be revealed.

The Good Lord doesn't tell you what his plan is, so all you can do is get up in the morning and see what happens next.
                                                          -- Richard Petty

**God chooses to keep much about himself
shrouded in mystery, but one day
we will see and we will understand.**

STRANGE BUT TRUE

Read 1 Corinthians 1:18-31.

"The message of the cross is foolishness to those who are perishing, but to us who are being saved it is the power of God" (v. 18).

As strange as it may sound, Ward Burton took the lead five laps from the finish of the 2002 Daytona 500 while he was sitting with his engine shut off.

Six laps remained when Sterling Marlin, running in ninth place, rear-ended Michael Waltrip and set off a chain reaction. The drivers in front of the wreck assumed that "the race would end under the ensuing yellow flag, meaning that whoever got to the start-finish line on this lap would be the winner." In a frantic effort to get there first, Marlin tried to duck under the leader, Jeff Gordon, who dropped down to block him but instead clipped Marlin's car and spun out of contention.

Marlin and Burton then sprinted to the finish with Marlin winning by inches. The race was apparently over. Officials decided, however, to pull out the red flag, meaning "the outcome would be determined by real racing."

After that final-lap sprint, however, Marlin removed a piece of sheet metal from his right front tire, a souvenir of the collision with Gordon; otherwise, he couldn't finish. Fender bending was against the rules, though, and Marlin was penalized by being dropped to the tail end of the lead lap.

NASCAR

Burton, who had apparently finished second and was sitting on the backstretch "as still as a gridlocked commuter on I-95" only a few feet away from Marlin, thus took the lead when racing began again. Elliott Sadler's second-place car couldn't make a serious run at him, so Burton held on and won this strange-but-true Daytona 500.

Life is just strange, isn't it? How else to explain the college bowl situation, Dr. Phil, tattoos, curling, tofu, and teenagers? Isn't it strange that today we have more ways to stay in touch with each other yet are losing the intimacy of personal contact?

And how strange is it that God let himself be killed by being nailed to a couple of pieces of wood? Think about that: the creator and ruler of the entire universe suffering the indignity and the torture that he did. And he did it quite willingly; this was God, after all. It's not like he wasn't capable of changing the course of events -- but he didn't. Isn't that strange?

But there's more that's downright bewildering. The cross, a symbol of disgrace, defeat, and death, ultimately became a worldwide symbol of hope, victory, and life. That's really strange. So is the fact that love drove God to that cross. It's strange – but it's true.

Every time someone asks about Pocono they say, 'That's a weird racetrack,' so I guess I just like weird.

-- *Darrell Waltrip*

Many things in life are strange, including God's allowing himself to be killed on a cross; but it's true, and it's because of his great love for you.

RESPECTFULLY YOURS

Read Mark 8:31-38.

*"He then began to teach them that the Son of Man must
suffer many things and be rejected by the elders, chief
priests and teachers of the law, and that he must be killed"*
(v. 31).

After Dale Jarrett drove his final competitive laps at Bristol
Motor Speedway on March 16, 2008, he took more than just a
bunch of memories with him into retirement. He took the respect
and admiration of his peers.

Jarrett's career spanned 25 years and included 32 wins, 163
top fives, and 260 top tens in NASCAR's Sprint Cup series. He
won three Daytona 500s and was the Cup champion in 1999. But
mere wins and statistics don't earn drivers what Jarrett received
at Bristol on his retirement day when the forty-two other drivers
and crew chiefs gave him a standing ovation during the pre-race
driver meetings.

"I have a lot of respect for Dale Jarrett," Matt Kenseth said. "I
think everybody out there does." "He is respectful to race with,"
declared Kevin Harvick. "You race him clean because he races
you clean."

Ned Jarrett waved the green flag on his son's final start and
declared Dale to be "a better race car driver than I was."

But Jarrett was an admirable representative of the sport outside
the track, too. NASCAR President Mike Helton said of Jarrett

at his retirement that he had been "a great ambassador, a great person, a classic role model for many of us in the sport."

In his final race, Jarrett finished a disappointing 37th, but as he said, "I really can't be too upset when you take into consideration the kind of career I have been fortunate enough to have."

Dale Jarrett had earned his wins, but he had also earned something much more important and much rarer: respect.

Rodney Dangerfield made a good living as a comedian with a repertoire that was basically only countless variations on one punch line: "I don't get no respect." Dangerfield was successful because he struck a chord with his audience. No one wants to be regarded by his peers with a total lack of respect. You want the respect, the esteem, and the regard that you feel you've earned.

But more often than not, you don't get it. Still, you shouldn't feel too badly; you're in good company. In the ultimate example of disrespect, Jesus – the very Son of God -- was treated as the worst type of criminal. He was arrested, bound, scorned, ridiculed, spit upon, tortured, condemned, and executed.

God allowed his son to undergo such treatment because of his high regard and his love for you. You are respected by almighty God! Could anyone else's respect really matter?

I have always respected Dale Jarrett as a competitor. To me he is just one of the greatest guys that you will ever meet.

-- *Jeff Gordon*

**You may not get the respect you deserve,
but at least nobody's spitting on you and
driving nails into you as they did to Jesus.**

HERO WORSHIP

Read 1 Samuel 16:1-13.

"Do not consider his appearance or his height, for . . . the Lord does not look at the things man looks at. . . . The Lord looks at the heart" (v. 7).

Tiny Lund won the 1963 Daytona 500 in a car he drove only because he had been a hero earlier in the week.

To make a little extra money, Marvin Panch agreed to test-drive a Maserati at Daytona. The car didn't feel right, so he took it easy. But Panch knew that Bill France had a standing offer of $10,000 for the first driver to post a speed of more than 180 miles per hour, and he figured this would be a good time to try for it. So he had some adjustments made to the car and headed back onto the track.

Heading into the third turn, the car suddenly went airborne. It landed on its side, rolled over onto its top, and slid along the track, bursting into flames along the way. Panch was trapped inside, and no matter how hard he kicked he could not budge the doors, which opened at the top and were jammed. Firemen arrived quickly, but they couldn't contain the blaze. Panch later said he seriously thought he wasn't going to make it and wondered what was going to happen to his wife and children.

Lund and four others who had witnessed the crash came over to see if they could help. They could. They lifted the car enough for Panch to kick open the door, but as Panch scrambled to escape, the gas tank exploded. They had to drop the car.

The flames intensified, and finally Lund and Steve Petrasek, a Firestone engineer, ran into the fire "with total disregard for their own safety. Lund grabbed Panch by one of his legs and jerked him out of and away from the car. Petrasek went temporarily blind as a result of his heroic effort." They saved Panch's life.

Lund had been looking for a ride, and now Panch's car was available. Lund not only drove, but in true heroic fashion, he won the race.

A hero is commonly thought of as someone who performs brave and dangerous feats that save or protect someone's life – like Tiny Lund and Steve Petrasek. You figure that excludes you.

But ask your son about that when you show him how to bait a hook, or your daughter when you show up for her dance recital. Look into the eyes of those Little Leaguers you help coach.

Ask God about heroism when you're steady in your faith. For God, a hero is a person with the heart of a servant. And if a hero is a servant who acts to save other's lives, then the greatest hero of all is Jesus Christ.

God seeks heroes today, those who will proclaim the name of their hero – Jesus – proudly and boldly, no matter how others may scoff or ridicule. God knows heroes when he sees them -- by what's in their hearts.

Sometimes the hero is built up to be torn down.
                                                      -- Dale Earnhardt, Jr.

**God's heroes are those who remain steady
in their faith while serving others.**

DAY 89

ULTIMATE MAKEOVER

Read 2 Corinthians 5:11-21.

"If anyone is in Christ, he is a new creation; the old has gone, the new has come!" (v. 17)

Many of the drivers of an earlier era probably couldn't make it in today's NASCAR -- but not because of how well they could drive a car.

"In the late sixties, stock car racing was still a small clique of devoted drivers, mechanics, and friends," wrote Peter Golenbock. "The prize money was still small, and those in it ran because it was in their blood." Drivers and mechanics often ate together and shared rooms together to save money. "People would lend other people gears or hubs or axles or whatever they needed, 'cause we were all in the same family, just a bunch of gypsies going up and down the highway," recalled Bob Latford, the designer of the points system.

For the drivers, that all changed in the early seventies when sponsors began paying big-time money to advertise on the cars. "From then on," said Golenbock, "it wasn't enough to be a great driver. You had to be a PR man as well." When the race was over, drivers had to make themselves over into public-relations men to represent the sponsors at meetings and shows. "The days of the scraggly, roughneck race driver were coming to an end."

Latford, who died in 2003, once reminisced that one of the "old school" drivers who probably "couldn't get a ride now because

NASCAR

all he could do was drive" was Bobby Isaac. Latford recalled that when Isaac started out, he won a race at Columbia Speedway, and "he went and hid in the infield because he was afraid people would want his autograph, and he didn't know how to sign his name." Isaac "couldn't have gone to a national sales meeting and talked to customers. There were a lot of drivers like that," drivers who couldn't or wouldn't make themselves over into PR men, a necessity in today's sport.

Ever considered a makeover? TV shows have shown us how changes in clothes, hair, and makeup and some weight loss can radically alter the way a person looks. But these changes are only skin deep. The real you — the person inside — remains unchanged. How can you make over that part of you?

By giving your heart and soul to Jesus -- just as you give up your hair to the makeover stylist. You won't look any different; you won't dance any better; you won't suddenly start talking smarter. The change is on the inside where you are brand new because the model for all you think and feel is now Jesus. He is the one you care about pleasing.

Made over by Jesus, you realize that gaining his good opinion — not the world's — is all that really matters. And he isn't the least interested in how you look but how you act.

A lot of drivers could work on cars and drive them, but they didn't want any part of the PR and the appearances.

-- Bob Latford

**Jesus is the ultimate makeover artist; he can make
you over without changing the way you look.**

LEFT BEHIND

Read Luke 18:18-29.

"No one who has left home or wife or brothers or parents or children for the sake of the kingdom of God will fail to receive many times as much in this age and, in the age to come, eternal life" (vv. 29-30).

In 2008, NASCAR finally and completely left behind its stock car roots.

In founding NASCAR, Bill France, Sr.'s stroke of brilliance that permanently altered the landscape of American sports was his conviction that the cars in all NASCAR events should be late-model vehicles. France staked his future and his fortune on his belief that race fans would be most interested in watching cars that looked like the ones they could buy in showrooms. Fans' loyalty would lie with the model as much as with the driver. Thus, when NASCAR began in 1949, "race cars were practically driven from the dealer's lots to the track."

But automakers quickly realized that wins on Sunday helped sell cars on Monday, so they began to build street cars that looked like race cars instead of the other way around. The catch was that NASCAR's rules still required a model to be available to the public to qualify as a stock car, so a minimum number had to be sold. The exact number varied; for instance, two hundred Chevrolet Monte Carlo Aerocoupes had to be sold to qualify it as a stock car.

NASCAR

In the first race of 2008, the Daytona 500, NASCAR officially put that era behind it with the introduction of the Car of Tomorrow. For the first time, a single car shape was used by all teams at all races. This generic body had nothing to do with the stock models in showrooms; it was now specifically designed for NASCAR competition.

At some time in your life, you have left loved ones, friends, and family behind. Your new job meant relocating, so you had to say goodbye to those neighbors who helped you raise your children. You left your family to go to school or into the service. To buy your new car, you traded in your beloved jalopy. The phases of your life are often measured by what you left behind.

The truth is we are often careless about not just the things but the people we leave behind. We are perhaps equally careless about what we say we would never leave behind.

But consider this question: What in your life would you leave everything else for? Your home, job, family, friends, wealth -- everything.

As with so many of life's questions, the only truly correct answer is Jesus. He demands that level of commitment; if he asks it, you must be willing to leave everything else behind for him.

I owe these guys a lot and it's tough for me to get up and leave. I'm not going to have the opportunity to race with them anymore and that's the bummer part of the deal.
-- David Reutimann on leaving the Darrell Waltrip Motorsports team

Your commitment to Jesus should be so total that you are willing to leave behind whatever he asks of you, knowing that greater rewards lie ahead.

NASCAR

NOTES
(by Devotion Day Number)

1   Bootleggers racing in a field . . . start of stock car racing.": Peter Golenbock, *The Last Lap Updated* (New York, Hungry Minds, Inc., 2001), p. 15.

1   "You could buy liquor legal, . . . to buy government liquor,": Golenbock, *The Last Lap*, p. 14.

1   Flock never hauled any liquor . . . and built some half-mile tracks.: Golenbock, *The Last Lap*, p. 15.

1   Racing cars began the day they built the second automobile.: Joe Menzer, *The Wildest Ride* (New York: Touchstone, 2001), p. 57.

2   "one of the most frustrating streaks ever in NASCAR history.": Jerry Bonkowski, "Most Memorable Daytona 500: No. 1 -- Dale Wins," *Yahoo!Sports*, Feb. 14, 2008, http://sports/yahoo.com/nascar/news?slug=jb-countdown021508&prov=yhoo&type-lgns, March 4, 2008.

2   "The harder he tried, the more frustrated he became,": Bonkowski, "Most Memorable Daytona 500."

2   "a one-thousand-pound gorilla.": Menzer, p. 280.

2   a streak of ten 125-mile qualifying races in a row.: Menzer, p. 280.

2   One year Earnhardt was running . . . knocked out of the race. Menzer, pp. 280-81.

2   In 1986, he was leading . . . He finished fifth.: Menzer, p. 280.

2   In 1993, he again was . . . passed him for the win.: David Poole and Jim McLaurin, *"Then Junior Said to Jeff . . ."* (Chicago: Triumph Books, 2006), p. 137.

2   "had all but given up . . . whatever happened happened.": Bonkowski, "Most Memorable Daytona 500."

2   "Every crew member of every . . . he drove to victory lane.": Bonkowski, "Most Memorable Daytona 500."

2   Earnhardt did doughnuts . . . number three in the dirt.: Menzer, p. 281.

2   I've got that monkey off my back.: Menzer, p. 282.

3   Edwards discovered his love . . . they raced on the weekend.: Poole and McLaurin, p. 171.

3   He drove dirt-track modifieds . . . would need a driver," Poole and McLaurin, p. 172.

3   in 2003 Roush Racing . . . rookie of the year.: Poole and McLaurin, p. 173.

3   Everywhere I went . . . you ought to hire him.": Poole and McLaurin, p. 172.

4   "None of these present-day guys seem superstitious,": Tom Higgins, "No Green and No Peanuts No Longer the Rule," *Tom Higgins' Scuffs*, ThatsRacin. com, Sept. 19, 2007, http://blogs.thatsracin.com/scuffs/2007/09/index.html, March 4, 2008.

4   when racing pioneer Louise Smith . . . the only car she had.: Peter Golenbock, *NASCAR Confidential* (St. Paul, MN: Motorbooks International, 2004), p. 14.

4   Joe Weatherly refused to run . . . green cars were taboo in NASCAR.: Higgins, "No Green and No Peanuts."

4   Most of the drivers decades . . . to being superstitious.: Higgins, "No Green and No Peanuts."

5   "incredible, 'Only-in-America" . . . sounding like Gomer Pyle": Tom Higgins, "Bill Elliott Was Well up to the Long Journey," *Tom Higgins' Scuffs*, ThatsRacin. com, Nov. 29, 2007, http://blogs.thatsracin.com/scuffs/2007/11/index.html, March 4, 2008.

5   "It has been a long road,": Higgins, "Bill Elliott."

5   Lordy, who would have ever thought it would come to this?: Higgins, "Bill Elliott."

6   On June 21, 1953, six Jaguars . . . moving up to Cup competition.: Steven Cole Smith, "NASCAR Fans: Be Careful When You Talk 'Tradition,'" *Edmunds Inside Line*, Feb. 16, 2007, http://www.edmunds.com/insideline/do/Columns/articleId=119633, April 6, 2008.

6   When I came along, I . . . racing Toyotas one day.: Eric Zweig, **** (Buffalo, NY: Firefly Books, 2007), p. 71. (See note in bibliography listing.)

7   three ways to do things: . . . was above and beyond.": Golenbock, *NASCAR Confidential*, p. 226.

7   moving to North Carolina in 1979 with fifty bucks and a 1966 Corvette.: Golenbock, *NASCAR Confidential*, p. 225.

7   Pemberton believed his chance . . . stopped by to eat.: Golenbock, *NASCAR Confidential*, p. 224.

7   Richard Petty "remembered the group . . . the opportunity based on that." Golenbock, *NASCAR Confidential*, p. 225.

7   "When I arrived, . . . Richard was very much the King.": Golenbock, *NASCAR Confidential*, p. 226.

7   They taught him "you don't . . . goal of winning the race.": Golenbock, *NASCAR Confidential*, p. 226.

7   The Petty way taught you . . . yourself or the company.: Golenbock, *NASCAR Confidential*, p. 226.

8   The race marked the first . . . to prove the "experts" wrong.: Poole and McLaurin, p. 27.

8   When Baker wrecked, the first . . had his head cut off.: Poole and McLaurin, p. 28.

8   Most of the drivers had taken . . . jug of cold tomato juice.: Poole and McLaurin, p. 27.

8   Other than being covered with . . . Baker was unhurt.: Poole and McLaurin, p. 28.

8   Wonder if they have boiled peanuts in California.: Monte Dutton, *** (New York: Warner Books, 2006), p. 7. (See note in bibliography listing.)

9   "I was livid . . . Then I prayed.": David Poole, "Helton Turned Life into Lessons," *Life in the Turn Lane*, March 31, 2008, http://turn-lane.blogspot.com, April 7, 2008.

9   I don't know why they . . . settle it outside the racetrack.: Zweig, p. 31.

10   he drove in cowboy boots . . . swollen feet and the hot boots.: Sam Moses, "Dick Trickle Is NASCAR's Newest Good Ol' Boy," *Sports Illustrated*, Dec. 11, 1989. http://vault.sportsillustrated.cnn.com/vault/article/magazine/MAG1069208/index.htm, March 21, 2008.

10   Trickle also drilled a hole . . . smoking as he raced.: "Dick Trickle." *Wikipedia, the free encyclopedia.* http://en.wikipedia.org/wiki/Dick_Trickle, March 21, 2008.

10   "possibly the most experienced . . . life is feeling good": Moses, "Dick Trickle."

10   The car doesn't know how old you are.: Zweig, p. 15.

11   In his interview, Bonnett spoke . . . belong to Neil Bonnett.": Tom Higgins, "An Australian Adventure, Part V," *Tom Higgins' Scuffs*, ThatsRacin.com, March 18, 2008, http://blogs.thatsracin.com/scuffs/2008/03/an-australian-1.html, April 1, 2008.

12   "toughest breed of people I have seen in my entire life.": Golenbock, *The Last Lap*, p. 90.

12   His "dad had an old . . . how tough can you get?": Golenbock, *The Last Lap*, p. 90.

12   "He made me mean, . . . the race even started.": Golenbock, *The*

Last Lap, p. 92.

12   "was probably as tough . . . met in my life." Golenbock, The Last Lap, p. 94.

12   Didn't come no tougher than him.": Golenbock, The Last Lap, p. 96.

12   At the Greenville-Pickens . . . "cut you with a knife." Golenbock, The Last Lap, p. 94.

12   The people in that era . . . with a tire iron.: Golenbock, The Last Lap, p. 98.

13   Curtis Tanner won more than . . . to finish the track.: Golenbock, NASCAR Confidential, p. 105.

13   Bill France responded by banning him from NASCAR in 1961.: Golenbock, NASCAR Confidential, p. 107.

13   "a whirlwind of fun and adventure.": Golenbock, NASCAR Confidential, p. 106.

13   "didn't even get grocery money" out of his father's estate.: Golenbock, NASCAR Confidential, p. 164.

13   "It was so bad that . . . something into the house,": Golenbock, NASCAR Confidential, p. 165.

13   His sister and he became . . . He found Jesus Christ": Golenbock, NASCAR Confidential, p. 166.

13   Tough times are the . . . me to be strong.: Zweig, p. 134.

14   "If you wanted to have . . . a way of life for us.": Menzer, p. 58.

14   "It was hard, dangerous, and scary work, . . . where I came from.": Menzer, pp. 58-59.

14   Their house was raided . . . stashes of illegal liquor.: Menzer, p. 59.

15   Had not NASCAR leveled . . . when they changed it like that,": Tom Jensen, "Jeff Gordon: Chasing Shadows," SPEEDtv.com, Nov. 17, 2007, http://nascar.speedtv.com/article/jeff_gordon_chasing_shadows, April 19, 2008.

15   As long as it's the same . . . theory is still the same.: Zweig, p. 41.

16   Judge grew up loved . . . not part of that crowd.": Golenbock, NASCAR Confidential, p. 83.

16   in 1958, when she was 21 . . . and they just danced.: Golenbock, NASCAR Confidential, p. 84.

16   In February 1959, a college . . . She told him he was right.: Golenbock, NASCAR Confidential, p. 85.

16   "I was hooked. That was it.": Golenbock, NASCAR Confidential, p. 86.

16   "I knew he loved me . . . waders for Christmas.": Golenbock, NASCAR Confidential, p. 88.

17   He built a reputation as . . . We, as a family, must have closure.": Becca Gladden, "The Rossi Files: The Life and Mysterious Death of a NASCAR Hero," Sports Illustrated, Sept. 13, 2007, http://sportsillustrated.cnn.com/2007/writers/the_bonus/09/11/nascar/index.html, April 19, 2008.

17   Nothing we do can bring . . . what we do moving forward.: Bruce Martin, "NASCAR's Official Accident Report -- No. 3 Car," hotrod.com, http://www.hotrod.com/thehistoryof/nascar_accident-report_dale_earnhardt/index.html, April 21, 2008.

18   Mundy drove a 1949 . . . turns at such high speeds.": Golenbock, NASCAR Confidential, p. 21.

18   In April 1951, Mundy towed . . . on France's private plane.: Golenbock, NASCAR Confidential, p. 46.

18   Years, ago, you used to . . . Those were the good old days.: Zweig, p. 59.

19   early on he was fascinated . . . was looking for help.: Golenbock, The Last Lap, p. 239.

19   So he drove down to . . . a career was launched.: Golenbock, The Last Lap, pp. 242.

19   "What do you want . . . going to make it.": Golenbock, *The Last Lap*, p. 242.

20   including affixing Allision's No. 28 . . . had done in 1985: Poole and McLaurin, p. 117.

20   Allison was in contention . . . those skies were threatening.: Poole and McLaurin, pp. 117-18.

20   McReynolds knew that if rain . . . green everywhere around us.": Poole and McLaurin, p. 118.

20   Few things are worse than a NASCAR rain delay.: Monte Dutton, "When Television Rained on the Viewers," *enctoday.com*, Feb. 29, 2008, http://www.enctoday.com/articles/nascar_5133_article.html/rain_fox.html, April 1, 2008.

21   Overton ran in the local . . . and wear the T-shirts.: Menzer, p. 72.

21   Overton had to badger his dad . . . racing nut ever since.": Menzer, p. 73.

21   "there was not much . . . to be around racing.": Menzer, p. 74.

21   drove "his parents nuts . . . I'd do all that stuff.": Menzer, p. 74.

21   If it had anything to do . . . I wanted to go.: Menzer, p. 74.

22   he went through his . . . thirteen cents he had borrowed.: Sam Moses, "Nice Meetin' Ya, The Name's Cale," *Sports Illustrated*, Nov. 6, 1978, http://vault.sportsillustrated.com/vault/article/magazine/MAG1094277/index.htm, March 21, 2008.

22   One time Buck Baker . . . a hot dog and a Coke.: Zweig, p. 114.

23   He confessed he wrestled . . . that had taken his life.: Menzer, p. 302.

23   On Sept. 7, 1998, he pulled in . . . under the car and was killed.: Menzer, pp. 299-300.

23   Adam turned to his . . . pick up and move on.: Menzer, p. 300.

23   "Part of living is dying," . . . we wanted him to.": Menzer, p. 302.

23   "Racing is what we know . . . got to make a living,": Menzer, p. 303.

23   You don't quit. You just keep plugging along.: Menzer, p. 303.

24   "a gathering place for guys . . . We won the race.": Golenbock, *NASCAR Confidential*, p. 212.

24   "We got up and went back . . . what was going on,": Golenbock, *NASCAR Confidential*, p. 212.

24   "That was a little, half-mile . . . give the victory trophy back.: Golenbock, *NASCAR Confidential*, pp. 213.

24   You can take all the . . . comes with the championship.: Zweig, p. 35.

25   The start of the 2007 NASCAR . . . a dream kind of season.: Lars Anderson, "Jimmie Stands Alone," *Sports Illustrated*, Dec. 5, 2007, http://vault.sportsillustrated.cnn.com/vault/article/magazine/MAG1115868/index.htm, March 22, 2008.

26   "famously arbitrary," playing . . . different than another guy.": Monte Dutton, "NASCAR Double Standard?" *enctoday.com*. May 22, 2007, http://www.enctoday.com/articles/stewart_4250_article.html/nascar-edwards.html, April 1, 2008.

26   It's a matter of what mood . . . to be honest with you.: Dutton, "NASCAR Double Standard?"

27   "Deep within, every race drivers harbors . . . and didn't say a word.: Tom Higgins, "Even with 10 Grand in Bodywork, the Gray Ghost Was Worth It," *Tom Higgins' Scuffs*, ThatsRacin.com, Feb. 7, 2006, http://blogs.thatsracin.com/scuffs/2006/02/even_with_10_gr.html, March 4, 2008.

27   Ya gotta wanna.: Zweig, p. 56.

28   Lee Petty recalled that . . . masked as pit crew members.": Sean Pantellere, "Pit Crew Renaissance," *Auto Racing Scene*, March 2, 2007, http://www.autoracingscene.com/articles_030207_pit_crew_renaissance, April 7, 2008.

28   Making better pit stops . . . testing, trying to get better.: Zweig, p. 154.

29   "loved racing as much as . . . the locals in Nashville.: Poole and McLaurin, pp. 13-14.

29   He never had enough money . . . lost more than $1,000.: Poole

	and McLaurin, p. 14.
29	He also said it was . . . when he blew by them.: Poole and McLaurin, p. 14.
29	We've got to conduct ourselves . . . conduct ourselves with integrity.: Zweig, p. 47.
30	Earles was one of . . . the founding of NASCAR.: Golenbock, *NASCAR Confidential*, p. 3.
30	He loved racing so much . . . the sanctioning body called NASCAR: Golenbock, *NASCAR Confidential*, p. 4.
30	and Earles changed his mind: Golenbock, *NASCAR Confidential*, pp. 4-5.
30	His first race was . . . helped France run NASCAR.: Golenbock, *NASCAR Confidential*, p. 5.
30	the sixth race was held at Martinsville.: Golenbock, *NASCAR Confidential*, p. 7.
30	Earles had 6,013 people . . . twelve thousand people.: Golenbock, *NASCAR Confidential*, p. 8.
30	I always put a lot . . . don't do enough thinking.: Golenbock, *NASCAR Confidential*, p. 8.
31	who was "fussing and fighting, mostly over money": Golenbock, *NASCAR Confidential*, p. 325.
31	As McReynolds recalled it . . . At the last moment, though,: Golenbock, *NASCAR Confidential*, p. 332.
31	Martin figured out what . . . as did Irvan.: Golenbock, *NASCAR Confidential*, p. 333.
31	I have a trick. . . . reflecting on my shirt.: Darren Rovell, "Carl Edwards Could Be Next Big Star of NASCAR," *CNBC.com*, March 10, 2008, http://www.cnbc.com/id/23557255, April 21, 2008.
32	"I was brought up not . . . my heroes were all in racing.": Golenbock, *The Last Lap*, p. 100.
32	He called it "pretty spooky" . . . "almost floored" his son.: Golenbock, *The Last Lap*, p. 101.
32	"See that old car in the corner over there?: Golenbock, *The Last Lap*, pp. 101-02.
32	Get you some people and. . . and you can run this weekend.": Golenbock, *The Last Lap*, p. 102.
32	"I got a little bit wide . . . was my own father!": Golenbock, *The Last Lap*, p. 102.
32	"I always respected . . . of finishing ahead of him.": Golenbock, *The Last Lap*, p. 108.
32	My father was my all-time special person.: Golenbock, *The Last Lap*, p. 100.
33	In 1984, U.S. Tobacco Co. . . . They're chasing me!": Poole and McLaurin, pp. 21-22.
33	I can't go fishing in my own lake . . . It's Neil's pond.: Poole and McLaurin, p. 126.
34	By 1967, though, he had . . . he retired for good.: Menzer, p. 217.
34	In his later years, Lorenzen . . . at 150 miles an hour.": "Fred Lorenzen," *Wikipedia, the free encyclopedia*, http://en.wikipedia.org/wiki/Fred_Lorenzen, April 2, 2008.
34	Looking back now . . . when I was young and dumb.: Larry Lage, "NASCAR's Mayfield Regrets Decisions When He Was 'Young and Dumb,'" *DailyJournalOnline Sports*, Aug. 23, 2007, http://www.mydjconnection.com/articles/2007/08/23/sports/doc46cda9a7578902889655712.txt, April 2, 2008.
35	Higgins had waited with Allison . . . in memory of Davey Allison.": Tom Higgins, "A Scene Seared in Memory," *Tom Higgins' Scuffs*, ThatsRacin.com, Sept. 12, 2007, http://blogs.thatsracin.com/scuffs/2007/09/index.html, March 4, 2008.
35	I want people to remember . . . doing something he loved.: Golenbock, *The Last Lap*, p. 382.

36 "built like a tank.": Menzer, p. 99.
36 Legendary car builder Edwin . . . because of his thick glasses.: "Drivers: Edwin Keith 'Banjo' Matthews," *LegendsofNASCAR.com*, http:www.legendsofnascar. com/Banjo_Matthews.htm, March 15, 2008.
36 Henry "Smokey" Yunick, so named . . . smoked up the track.: Menzer, p. 143.
36 whose strategy was to build . . . and collect his winnings.: Steve Samples, "Herman the Turtle," *Beyond the Grandstand*, Jan. 2, 2002, http://www.gordon-line.com/beyond/010202.html, March 5, 2008.
36 H.A. "Humpy" Wheeler acquired his . . . run laps as punishment.: Menzer, p. 81.
36 "Suitcase" Jake Elder was nicknamed . . . tendency to change teams.: Golenbock, *The Last Lap*, p. 199.
36 "Chargin' Charlie" Glotzbach, nicknamed for his driving style?: "Charlie Glotzbach," *Cotton Owens Garage*, http://www.cottonowens.com/charlie_glotz bach.html, March 15, 2008.
36 The idea that someone . . . repugnant to me." Golenbock, *NASCAR Confidential*, p. 85.
37 a Connecticut Yankee who decided . . . worse than any injury in a car wreck.": Tom Higgins, "Daytona by the Decades," *Tom Higgins' Scuffs*, ThatsRacin.com. Jan. 9, 2008, http://blogs.thatsracin.com/scuffs/2008/01/index.html, March 4, 2008.
37 Judging by some of . . . I feel like I'm 18.: Zweig, p. 13.
38 "A hundred years from now . . . driver that's ever been.": Golenbock, *The Last Lap*, p. 334.
38 When NASCAR raced in Japan in 1996, he was mobbed for autographs.: Golenbock, *The Last Lap*, p. 331.
38 when the Richard Childress racing team . . . blew up and was gone.: Golenbock, *The Last Lap*, p. 335.
38 I would like to thank . . . and your last names.: Zweig, p. 85.
39 "far-reaching, far-thinking . . . in showrooms across America.": Golenbock, *The Last Lap*, p. 1.
39 "master politician with a great sense of timing," Golenbock, *The Last Lap*, p. 139.
39 a "benevolent dictator,": Golenbock, *The Last Lap*, p. 140.
39 "on balance . . . was a genius.": Golenbock, *The Last Lap*, p. 141.
39 When deposed dictator Fulgencio Batista fled . . . Batista and Bill France.": Golenbock, *The Last Lap*, pp. 139-40.
39 "had the vision and drive . . . and more in his NASCAR career.": Steve McCormick, "Bill France Jr.," *About.com: NASCAR Racing*, http://nascar.about.com/od/nascarhistory/p/billfrancejr.htm, March 1, 2008.
39 The modern era of NASCAR . . . to a worldwide phenomenon." Mark Aumann, "Bill France Jr. Dies at 74," *NASCAR.com*, June 5, 2007, http://www.nascar. com/2007/news/headlines/cup/06/04/bfrancejr.dies.obit/index.html, March 1, 2008.
39 Bill France, Sr. was the architect . . . the ultimate general manager.: Aumann.
40 he set a record: "Ned Jarrett," *Wikipedia, the free encylopedia*, http://en.wikipedia. org/wiki/Ned_Jarrett, Sept. 4. 2009.
40 the track where he had . . . didn't want to go to college.: Poole and McLaurin, p. 90.
40 The younger Jarrett was charged . . . for use in demolition derbies.: Poole and McLaurin, p. 91.
40 Before a driver starts asking . . . much of the problem is him.: Zweig, p. 158.
41 Yarborough once dumped a bucket . . . damage to Yarborough's

head.: Jeff Alan, "The Good Ole Days -- Part 3," *Jeff Alan's NASCAR Racing Commentary*, http://members.aol.com/jalan5000a/com0044.html, April 7, 2008.

41 It's been so tough . . . me get through it.: "Texas: Toyota NASCAR Nationwide Race Racap, Quotes," *PaddockTalk*, April 5, 2008, http://www.paddocktalk.com/news/html, April 7, 2008.

42 they'd have to name it *Gone with the Wind*: Poole and McLaurin, p. 57.

42 Without a ride, Johnson . . . "bloody black art" of drafting.: Poole and McLaurin, p. 57.

42 A series of crashes . . . "I was long gone.": Poole and McLaurin, p. 58.

42 Keep working and try. . . . to be doing something anyhow.: Zweig, p. 133.

43 "season of torment": Mark Bechtel, "Just Racin'," *Sports Illustrated*, March 19, 2002. http://vault.sportsillustrated.ccn.com/vault/article/magazine/MAG 1025169/index.htm, March 26, 2008.

43 Marlin's "long dark ride" . . . did the furor subside.: Bechtel.

43 Earnhardt driver Michael Waltrip also . . . cleared him of any wrongdoing.: "Sterling Marlin," *Wikipedia, the free encyclopedia*, http://en.wikipedia.org/wiki/Sterling_Marlin, Sept. 9, 2009.

43 he couldn't make people talk . . . didn't do anything wrong.": Bechtel.

43 Second place is just the first loser.: Zweig, p. 131.

44 Parsons grew up . . . father could find work.: Menzer, p. 176.

44 His dad, Harold, introduced . . . during the summer.: Menzer, p. 177.

44 When he finished . . . those cabs running,": Menzer, p. 178.

44 One day in May . . . learned the racing business.: Menzer, p. 179.

44 It was totally by chance. . . . go to the bathroom.: Menzer, p. 179.

45 He once found himself . . . and he finished third.": Jeff Alan, "The Good Old Days -- Part I," *Jeff Alan's NASCAR Racing Commentary*, http://members.aol.com/jalan5000a/com0042.html, April 7, 2008.

45 Since racers ran regular . . . to put a monkey out of it.": Alan, "The Good Old Days – Part I."

45 I've always had a love . . . do things with them.: Kris Johnson, "Newmans Saving Lives of Dogs Across America, *Ryan Newman Foundation*, Feb. 19, 2008, http://www.ryannewmanfoundation.org/news/2008/02222008.htm, April 8, 2008.

46 "humble wisdom and no-frills . . ." promote driver-fan friendliness.: Alan Ross, "King Richard Rules," *AmericanProfile.com*, Jan. 30, 2005, http://www.americanprofile.com/article/4561.html, April 21, 2008.

46 He is widely considered the greatest NASCAR driver of all time.: "Richard Petty," *Wikipedia, the free encyclopedia*, http://en.wikipedia.org/wiki/Richard_Petty, April 22, 2008.

46 "My object was to win,": Ross.

46 "Get from Turn One . . . what it's all about.": Ross.

46 First you learn to . . . do it for 500 miles.: Zweig, p. 77.

47 "Shelmerdine was cut from . . . won more titles.": Poole and McLaurin, pp. 133-34.

47 Back in 1981, he went South . . . I was wired for it.": Poole and McLaurin, p. 133.

47 After saying good-bye to . . . with his old team.": Poole and McLaurin, p. 134.

47 I'm a full-blooded . . . a dream tickles me pink.: Zweig, p. 54.

48 If stock-car racing had a P.T. Barnum, it would be H.A. 'Humpy' Wheeler.": Poole and McLaurin, p. 100.

48 "vast contributions to racing": Menzer, p. 84.

48 His philosophy as a . . . was, literally, a circus.": Poole and McLaurin, p. 100.

48 After Cale Yarborough slapped . . . Holly Farms Poultry.: "H.A. Wheeler," *Wikipedia, the free encyclopedia*, http://en.wikipedia.org/wiki/Humpy_Wheeler,

48   March 5, 2008.

48   For a Coca-Cola 600 . . . started dropping from heat exhaustion.": Tom Higgins, "We're Having a Heat Wave," *Tom Higgins' Scuffs*, ThatsRacin.com, Aug. 7, 2007, http://blogs.thatsracin.com/scuffs/2007/08/index.html, March 4, 2008.

48   "They were dropping like flies,": Poole and McLaurin, p. 101.

48   The show must go on! The show must stop!: Higgins, "We're Having a Heat Wave."

49   "It was frightening to . . . someone like Fireball Roberts.": Menzer, p. 118.

49   In 1953, France pondered . . . racing had never seen.": Menzer, p. 113.

49   the grand finale: . . . about the high speeds: Menzer, p. 115.

49   "These guys will never survive this track.": Menzer, p. 116.

49   It was an awesome thing.": Menzer, p. 117.

49   sixty-one hours after the race was over.: Menzer, p. 120.

49   "There wasn't a man there who wasn't scared to death of it.": Menzer, p. 120.

49   Other tracks separate the men . . . after the boys are gone.: Menzer, p. 118.

50   "a long straightaway . . .dug deep into his cheek.": Earl Swift, "The Story Behind the Scar of Norfolk's Early NASCAR Hero," *The Virginian-Pilot*, Oct. 2, 2007, http://www.joeweatherly.com/Stories.htm, March 3, 2008.

50   In October 1946 in Norfolk, Va., . . . "and the tree was right there.": Swift.

50   Joe Weatherly's scar crossed . . . third of the smile behind,: Swift.

51   Joe Nemechek described the pressure on NASCAR drivers as "immense.": Zweig, p. 135.

51   Stewart had a comfortable lead . . . wedged between his knees.": Jerry Bonkowski, "Picture of Cool," *Yahoo!Sports*, July 29, 2007, http://sports.yahoo.com/nascar/news, April 3, 2008.

51   "treating what likely will be . . . didn't worry and didn't waver.": Bonkowski, "Picture of Cool."

52   In 1968 at a race in Columbia . . . Wanda from North Carolina.: Golenbock, *The Last Lap*, p. 259.

52   "I was not at all . . . I wanted to meet Buck Baker.": Golenbock, *The Last Lap*, p. 260.

52   When their paths crossed . . . he'd get the message.: Golenbock, *The Last Lap*, p. 261.

52   Lund "just happened" to show . . . for not listening to him.: Golenbock, *The Last Lap*, pp. 261-62.

52   To finish first, you must first finish.: Zweig, p. 166.

53   Epton's first experience with racing . . . She kept working.: Vincent M. Mallozzi, "Years of Thunder for Woman Called Lightning," *The New York Times*, Nov. 25, 2007, http://www.nytimes.com/2007/11/25/sports/othersports/25cheer.html, April 23, 2008.

54   Ford invited him to a party . . . put the engine together.: Menzer, p. 194.

54   Working at his dad's . . . a two-year-old child,: Menzer, p. 195.

54   "a frame with a body . . . 'Here you go.'": Menzer, p. 194.

54   "I didn't have the first clue . . . pole for the ARCA race.: Menzer, p. 195.

54   The impossible just took . . . we got it done.: Menzer, p. 195.

55   "Toward the end of a race, . . . quite, literally, death.": Kim Severson, "At 190 M.P.H., Who Needs a Spare Tire?" *The New York Times*, June 14, 2006, http://www.nytimes.com/2006/06/14/dining/14nasc.html, April 24, 2008.

55   "I ran a lot, but . . . fry it, I'll eat it.": Severson.

55   While he still sneaks . . . Now I love it.": Severson.

55   Tony Stewart once had his . . . frozen pepperoni pizza.: Severson.

55   Basically we NASCAR fans . . . we're proud of it.: Severson.

56   In 1972, rookie Darrell Waltrip . . . to win his first NASCAR race.:

Sam Moses, "If You Can't Prove It, You Ain't It," *Sports Illustrated*, Oct. 17, 1977, http://vault.sportsillustrated.cnn.com/vault/article/magazine/MAG1092910/index.htm, March 21, 2008.

56   "You had to prove . . . a chance to make it,": Lars Anderson, "Generation NEX-TEL," *Sports Illustrated*, Nov. 30, 2005, http://vault/sportsillustrated.cnn.com/vault/article/magazine/MAG1115866/index.htm, March 24, 2008.

56   In 1996, only three full-time . . . were younger than 30.: Jeremy Dunn, "The Rookie That Changed NASCAR," *Auto Racing Scene*, April 20, 2006, http://www.autoracingscene.com/042006rookie-that-changed-nascar, April 7, 2008.

56   the youngest driver ever to win a Cup race;: Anderson, "Generation NEXTEL."

56   the youngest national series champion in NASCAR history.: Anderson, "Generation NEXTEL."

56   When I came up . . . the way it is anymore.: Anderson, "Generation NEXTEL."

57   the first time Waltrip . . . to give him something to do.: Poole and McLaurin, pp. 66.

57   Johnson didn't really have . . . "balance" the tires, not bounce them.: Poole and McLaurin, pp. 67.

58   When your driver doesn't respond . . . to go over there.": Golenbock, *NASCAR Confidential*, p. 341.

58   his response was to throw up . . . . It can't be possible,": Golenbock, *NASCAR Confidential*, p. 342.

58   McReynolds prayed for God . . . suffer and be comatose.: Golenbock, *NASCAR Confidential*, p. 342.

58   The doctors gave Irvan less than a twenty percent chance of surviving.: Golenbock, *NASCAR Confidential*, p. 343.

58   Five days after the . . . survival were getting better.: Golenbock, *NASCAR Confidential*, p. 343.

58   Two weeks after the accident, . . . "I'm going to race.": Golenbock, *NASCAR Confidential*, p. 344.

58   In the late summer of 1995, rip the grandstand down.": Golenbock, *NASCAR Confidential*, p. 346.

58   No one would ever say . . . three-week period of time: Golenbock, *NASCAR Confidential*, p. 344.

59   Guthrie qualified 27th . . . and empty their trucks.: David Newton, "NASCAR No Place for Women . . . Until Guthrie," *NASCAR.com*, May 26, 2006, http://www.nascar.com/2006/news/headlines/cup/05/26/jguthrie.women.nascar/index.html, April 22, 2008.

59   I thought it was a nuclear . . . with their sirens going.: Newton.

60   The asphalt hadn't had time . . . chunks that flew everywhere.: Golenbock, *The Last Lap*, p. 219.

60   "The more Turner and . . . gallons of liquid rubber sealer.: Menzer, p. 127.

60   crews put bars and chicken wire . . . a steam locomotive cowcatcher.": Menzer, p. 128.

60   "The asphalt broke apart . . . the track had finished him.: Menzer, p. 129.

60   I don't believe anybody could finish this race in a tank.: Menzer, p. 127.

61   Johnson was among the leaders . . . 'Yeah, the whole run," he said.: "Johnson Breaks Through for First Win," *Sports Illustrated*, April 13, 2008, http://sportsillustrated.cnn.com/2008/racing/04/13/nascar.phoenix.ap/index.html, April 13, 2008.

61   "We do not choose . . . on which we will stand." R. Alan Culpepper, "The Gospel of Luke: Introduction, Commentary, and Reflections," *The New Interpreter's Bible* (Nashville: Abingdon Press, 1995), Vo. IX, p. 153.

NASCAR

61   The three things that helped me . . . family and my friends.: John Sturbin, "The NASCAR Super Team: Hendrick Motorsports," *Star-Telegram.com*, April 3, 2008, http://www.star-telegram.com/sports/story/561705.html, April 13, 2008.

62   In 1965 he showed up at Daytona . . . a putrid brown color that looked like --: Menzer, p. 201.

62   He thought he had won . . . picture taken in Victory Lane.": Menzer, p. 202.

62   Jeff Gordon came in wearing Nikes while everyone else was wearing cowboy boots.: Raygan Swan, "Who Are You Wearing?" *NASCAR.com*, Feb. 22, 2008, http://www.hobbytalk.com.bbs1/showthread.php?t=211886, April 1, 2008.

63   the most "harebrained scheme" ever.: "Ned Jarrett," *howstuffworks.com*, http://entertainment.howstuffworks.com/ned-jarrett.htm, April 14, 2008.

63   he still couldn't convince . . . the check cleared the bank.: "Ned Jarrett."

63   We don't want to . . . that's never the plan.": "Sensational NASCAR Crash," *angrybrownguy.com*, April 5, 2008, http://www.angrybrownguy.com/?p=257, April 24, 2008.

64   "There was cheating going on from day one.": Menzer, p. 74.

64   Glenn Dunnaway led the 33-car . . . competitors needed a hand.": Menzer, p. 75.

65   The ceremony on Feb. 22, . . . it was over.: "NASCAR Mourns The Intimidator," *CBSNews.com*, Feb. 22, 2001, http://www.cbsnews.com/stories/2001/02/21/sports/main273652, Feb. 22, 2008.

66   In 1967, Baker was leading . . . "I'm going to kill you.": Poole and McLaurin, pp. 52-53.

66   It was the dustiest place . . . had dropped a bomb.: Zweig, p. 58.

67   "go racing Grand National": Golenbock, *The Last Lap*, p. 154.

67   Pearson started driving when , . . . his brother's body shop. Golenbock, *The Last Lap*, p. 152.

67   "because I had always been . . . "It was a lot of fun.": Golenbock, *The Last Lap*, p. 153.

67   making more money than . . . for him to buy a car: Golenbock, *The Last Lap*, p. 154.

67   working on his car under a tree . . . to get into Grand National racing.: Golenbock, *The Last Lap*, p. 154.

67   Racing cars is not the safest . . . not the sanest thing.: Zweig, p. 50.

68   His No. 22 Pontiac . . . knew the name Fireball Roberts.": Golenbock, *NASCAR Confidential*, p. 101.

68   "the first superstar.": Golenbock, *The Last Lap*, p. 129.

68   "a smart driver," . . . an excellent representative.": Golenbock, *The Last Lap*, p. 129.

68   Fireball Roberts was perhaps . . . all stock-car drivers.: Zweig, p. 168.

69   "a blue-collar, tight-knit . . . pursue his dream of racing.: Jerry Bonkowski, "The Family Guy Tackles Daytona," *Yahoo!Sports.com*, http://sports.yahoo.com/nascar/news, Feb 17, 2008.

69   especially for crew chief . . . pride in the stands.": Bonkowski.

70   In the early 1960s, Turner had . . . betting on the races.: Golenbock, *The Last Lap*, p. 217.

70   he signed up many . . . Bucker Baker, and Richard Petty.: Golenbock, *The Last Lap*, p. 220.

70   France called a meeting . . . the union reps disappeared,: Golenbock, *The Last Lap*, p. 221.

70   Turner's wife Bunny called France. . . what he had to do." Golenbock, *The Last Lap*, p. 234.

70   France reinstated Tuner and was a pallbearer at Turner's funeral.: Golenbock, *The Last Lap*, p. 234.

70   Curtis and Bill patched it up before Curtis's death.: Golenbock, *The Last Lap*, p. 234.

71   with Petty in 1967 at the top. Mark Ashenfelter, "Top 10 NASCAR Seasons," *ESPN.com: NextelCup*, Jan. 9, 2008, http://sports.espn.go.com/espn/print? id=3187989&type=story, March 4, 2008.

71   "We ran 48 races . . . not of his own making.: Tom Higgins, "A King Is Born," *Tom Higgins' Scuffs*. ThatsRacin.com. 24 Sept. 2007. http://blogs.thatsracin.com/ scuffs/2007/09/index.html, March 4, 2008.

71   Jeff Gordon in 1998 with . . . despite completing only 31 races.: Ashenfelter.

71   If everyone would just live . . . the world would be. Quoted on http://www. criminalgrace.com/obsessions/quotes.html.

72   Ten years before Bill France . . land suitable for a track.: Golenbock, *NASCAR Confidential*, p. 45.

72   On part of his land, . . . to avoid the minnow farm.: Golenbock, *NASCAR Confidential*, p. 45.

72   Indy car drivers quickly . . . They struck a deal,: Golenbock, *NASCAR Confidential*, p. 55.

72   I knew in my head . . . known better than that.: "Quotebook: Chase for the Nextel Cup Drivers." *NASCAR.com*, Oct. 31, 2004, http://www.nascar.com/ 2004/news/headlines/cup/10/31/atlanta_quotes.index.html, April 20, 2008.

73   The last race of the 2004 season . . . Tony now looks at solutions,": Lars Anderson, "Bringing It All Back Home," *Sports Illustrated*, Aug. 8, 2005, http:// vault.sportsillustrated.cnn.com/vault/article/magazine/MAG1108569/index. htm, March 24, 2008.

73   he was the first person . . . to a lifetime contract.": Anderson, "Bringing It All Back Home."

73   I always knew you'd come back . . . always give you shakes.: Anderson, "Bringing It All Back Home."

74   Start it up, drive it over the Grand Canyon, and jump out.": Golenbock, *The Last Lap*. pp. 247-48.

74   In January 1974, he . . . changing the motor.: Golenbock, *The Last Lap*, pp. 247-48.

74   When you're a driver and . . . give you a magical answer.: Dutton, ***, p. 79.

75   In 1961 at the Asheville-Weaverville . . . without any further incidents.: Poole and McLaurin, pp. 74-75.

75   I got out and he went to beating on my fist with his nose.: Menzer, p. 231.

76   Smith lived in South Carolina . . . She finished third.: Golenbock, *NASCAR Confidential*, p. 13.

76   France asked her to . . . "I tore that car up,": Golenbock, *NASCAR Confidential*, p. 14.

76   Not surprisingly, her husband . . . her racing after that.: Golenbock, *NASCAR Confidential*, p. 15.

76   In 1949, she bought . . . first official events.: Golenbock, *NASCAR Confidential*, p. 11.

76   Sara Christian and Ethel Mobley . . . the tracks in 1948: *Golenbock, NASCAR Confidential*, p. 17.

77   Taken by a fan and . . . a lap down and finished fifth.: Fairbank, Dave, "Inaugural Daytona 500 Photo Developed a Buzz," http://www.joeweatherly. com/Stories.htm, March 3, 2008.

77   That photograph right there propelled the sport into a new world.: Fairbank.

78   When Bill France announced . . . operating a team were skyrocketing.: Menzer, p. 198.

78   he was feeling the . . . with a Reynolds executive.: Menzer, p. 198.

78	who asked him how much . . . he contacted France.: Menzer, p. 199.
78	Reynolds sponsored its first race . . . in May 1971.: Menzer, p. 200.
78	There's no bigger surprise . . . getting hit from the rear.: Zweig, p. 50.
79	On May 24, 2007, the flag . . . postage stamp on it,": Vincent M. Mallozzi, "NASCAR Flag Is Planted at the Top of the World," *The New York Times*, Sept. 9, 2007, http://www.nytimes.com/2007/09/09/sports/othersports/09cheer.html, April 23, 2008.
79	The house if up there, but this is his home.: David Newton, "Junior Johnson Remains Active as a Father, Farmer," *NASCAR.com*, July 31, 2006, http://www. nascar.com/2006/news/features/lifestyle/07/31/junior.johnson/index.html, April 6, 2008.
80	"things were simpler . . . It was just wrong.": Dennis Burton, "Racing a Lifelong Passion," *Richmond County Daily Journal*, Aug. 4, 2007, http://lynyrdskynyrd dixie.com/forums/viewtopic.php?p=7564, April 17, 2008.
80	NASCAR has changed so . . . boys as you used to.: Zweig, p. 146.
81	When Flock pulled into the infield . . . beside his car to take a nap.: Golenbock, *The Last Lap*, p. 24.
81	a man was putting Champion . . . backing over my head.": Golenbock, *The Last Lap*, p. 25.
81	We just out thunk 'em there at the end.: Zweig, p. 159.
82	Earnhardt was the point leader . . . eighth in the final point standings.: "Dale Earnhardt," *Wikipedia, the free encyclopedia*, http://en.wikipedia.org/wiki/Dale_Earnhardt, Feb. 22, 2008.
82	Earnhardt "was a bummed up" . . . good two to three years.": Golenbock, *NASCAR Confidential*, p. 357.
82	Only after Earnhardt had surgery . . . he return to form.: Golenbock, *NASCAR Confidential*, p. 358.
82	You hit the wall head-on; it hurts.: Dutton, ***, p. 134.
83	the guys with the best . . . to keep a driver safe.": Jerry Bonkowski, "On the Constant Lookout," *Yahoo!Sports*, Feb. 16, 2008, http://sports.yahoo.com/nascar/news, April 3, 2008.
83	The spotters let the drivers . . . it's a great day." Bonkowski, "On the Constant Lookout."
83	Money may be the most . . . a very close second.: *billelliott.com*. http://www.billelliott.com/about/quotes.html, March 1, 2008.
84	Roberts decided to retire after the 1964 season. Golenbock, *NASCAR Confidential*, p. 121.
84	he signed a contract . . . commentary for NASCAR. Golenbock, *NASCAR Confidential*, p. 121.
84	His divorce was finalized . . . into the commentary business.": Golenbock, *NASCAR Confidential*, p. 133.
84	Roberts had three races . . . proved to be too much.: Golenbock, *NASCAR Confidential*, p. 134.
84	"I just didn't think it was going to happen,": Golenbock, *NASCAR Confidential*, p. 135.
84	In a race, what I fear most is fire.: Zweig, p. 168.
85	The reporter wrote a paragraph, . . . the information in his log.: Tom Higgins, "Metcalfe, Mark Maker," *Tom Higgins' Scuffs*, ThatsRacin.com, Sept. 4, 2007, http://blogs.thatsracin.com/scuffs/2007/09/index.html, March 4, 2008.
85	The Good Lord doesn't . . . see what happens next.: Zweig, p. 65.
86	Six laps remained when . . . a serious run at him,: Mark Bechtel, "Spin City," *Sports Illustrated*, Feb. 25, 2002, http://vault.sports illustrated.cnn.com/vault/article/magazine/MAG1024974/index.

86	htm, March 26, 2008.
	Every time someone asks . . . I just like weird.: Zweig, p. 161.
87	the forty-two other drivers and . . . the pre-race driver meetings.: Jenna Fryer, "Jarrett Honored Throughout the Industry Before Final Start," *Yahoo!Sports*, March 16, 2008, http://sports.yahoo.com/nascar/news, March 17, 2008.
87	"I have a lot of respect . . . because he races you clean.": Bob Margolis, "No Regrets," *Yahoo!Sports*, March 14, 2008, http://sports.yahoo.com/nascar/news, March 15, 2008.
87	Ned Jarrett waved the green . . . car driver than I was.": Fryer.
87	NASCAR President Mike Helton . . . fortunate enough to have.": Fryer.
87	I have always respected . . . that you will ever meet.: Margolis.
88	To make a little extra money, . . . a result of his heroic effort.": Menzer, pp. 144-45.
88	Sometimes the hero is built up to be torn down.: Marty Smith, "Junior: 'Sometimes the Hero is Built up to Be Torn Down,'" *NASCAR.com*, http://www.nascar.com/special/earnhardt/stories/interview.html, June 25, 2008.
89	"In the late sixties, stock car . . . it was in their blood.": Golenbock, *The Last Lap*, p. 173.
89	"People would lend other . . . up and down the highway,": Golenbock, *The Last Lap*, p. 175.
89	"From then on . . . coming to an end.": Golenbock, *The Last Lap*, p. 173.
89	"old school" drivers . . . a lot of drivers like that,": Golenbock, *The Last Lap*, p. 177.
89	A lot of drivers could work . . . the PR and the appearances.: Golenbock, *The Last Lap*, p. 177.
90	"race cars were practically driven . . . " specifically designed for NASCAR competition.: Jerry Garrett, "When Stock Meant Stock," *The New York Times*, Feb. 17, 2008, http://www.nytimes.com/2008/02/17/automobiles/collectibles/17speed.html, April 22, 2008.
90	I owe these guys a lot . . . the bummer part of the deal.: "Reutimann Says Goodbye to a Good Home in the NASCAR Craftsman Truck Series," *Toyota.com*, Nov. 13, 2006, http://toyota.com/motorsports/ncts/news/2006/11-13-06-01.html, April 22, 2008.

BIBLIOGRAPHY

Alan, Jeff. "The Good Old Days -- Part I." *Jeff Alan's NASCAR Racing Commentary*. http://members.aol.com/jalan5000a/com0042.html.

---. "The Good Old Days -- Part 3." *Jeff Alan's NASCAR Racing Commentary*. http://members.aol.com/jalan5000a/com0044.html.

Anderson, Lars. "Bringing It All Back Home." *Sports Illustrated*. 8 Aug. 2005. http://vault/sportsillustrated.ccn.com/vault/article/magazine/MAG1108569/index.htm.

---. "Generation NEXTEL." *Sports Illustrated*. 30 Nov. 2005. http://vault.sportsillustrated.cnn.com/vault/article/magazine/MAG1115866/index.htm.

---. "Jimmie Stands Along." *Sports Illustrated*. 5 Dec. 2007. http://vault.sportsillustrated.cnn.com/vault/article/magazine/MAG115868/index.htm.

Ashenfelter, Mark. "Top 10 NASCAR Seasons." *ESPN.com: NEXTEL Cup*. 9 Jan. 2008. http://sports.espn.go.com/espn/print?id=3187989&type=story.

Aumann, Mark. "Bill France Jr. Dies at 74." *NASCAR.com*. 5 June 2007. http://www.nascar.com/2007/news/headlines/cup/06/04/bfrancejr.dies.obit/index.html.

Bechtel, Mark. "Just Racin'." *Sports Illustrated*. 18 March 2002. http://vault.sportsillustrated. cnn.com/vault/article/magazine/MAG1025169/index.htm.
---. "Spin City." *Sports Illustrated*. 25 Feb 2002. http://vault.sportsillustrated.cnn.com/vault/ article/magazine/MAG1024974/index.htm.
Billelliott.com. http://www.billelliott.com/about/quotes.html.
Bonkowski, Jerry. "The Family Guy Tackles Daytona." *Yahoo!Sports.com*. 17 Feb. 2008. http:// sports/yahoo.com/nascar/news.
---. "Most Memorable Daytona 500: No. 1 -- Dale Wins." *Yahoo!Sports*. 14 Feb. 2008. http:// sports.yahoo.com/nascar/news.?slug=jb-countdown021508&prov+yhoo&type=lgns.
---. "On the Constant Lookout." *Yahoo!Sports*. 16 Feb. 2008. http://sports.yahoo.com/nascar/ news.
---. "Picture of Cool." *Yahoo!Sports*. 29 July 2007. http://sports.yahoo.com/nascar/news.
Burton, Dennis. "Racing a Lifelong Passion." *Richmond County Daily Journal*. 4 Aug. 2007. http://lynyrdskynyrddixie.com/forums/viewtopic.php?p=7564.
"Charlie Glotzbach." *Cotton Owens Garage*. http://www.cottonowens.com/charlie_glotzbach. html.
Criminal Grace. com. http://www.criminalgrace.com/obsessions/quotes.html.
Culpepper, R. Alan. "The Gospel of Luke: Introduction, Commentary, and Reflections." *The New Interpreter's Bible*. Nashville: Abingdon Press, 1995. Vol. IX, 1-490.
"Dale Earnhardt." *Wikipedia, the free encyclopedia*. http://en.wikipedia.org/wiki/Dale_ Earnhardt.
"Dick Trickle." *Wikipedia, the free encyclopedia*. http://en.wikipedia.org.wiki/Dick_Trickle.
"Drivers: Edwin Keith 'Banjo' Matthews." *LegendsofNASCAR.com*. http://www.legendsof nascar.com/Banjo_Matthews.htm.
Dunn, Jeremy. "The Rookie That Changed NASCAR." *Auto Racing Scene*. 20 April 2006. http://www.autoracingscene.com/042006rookie-that-changed-nascar.
Dutton, Monte. ***. New York: Warner Books, 2006. (The title is not suitable for publication here; for the book's title, contact the author.)
---. "NASCAR Double Standard? Why One Gets Parked and Another Gets a Pass." *enctoday.com*. 22 May 2007. http://www.enctoday.com/articles/stewart_4250_article. html/nascar_edwards.html.
---. "When Television Rained on the Viewers." *enctoday.com*. 29 Feb. 2008. http://www. enctoday.com/articles/nascar_5133_article.html/rain_fox.html.
Fairbank, Dave. "Inaugural Daytona 500 Photo Developed a Buzz." *JoeWeatherly.com*. http:// www.joeweatherly.com/Stories.htm.
"Fred Lorenzen." *Wikipedia, the free encylopedia*. http://en.wikipedia.org/wiki/Fred_ Lorenzen.
Fryer, Jenna. "Jarrett Honored Throughout the Industry Before Final Start." *Yahoo!Sports*. 16 March 2008. http://sports.yahoo.com/nascar/news.
Garrett, Jerry. "When Stock Meant Stock." *The New York Times*. 17 Feb. 2008. http://www. nytimes.com/2008/02/17/automobiles/collectibles/17speed.html.
Gladden, Becca. "The Rossi Files: The Life and Mysterious Death of a NASCAR Hero." *SI.com*. 13 Sept. 2007. http://sportsillustrated.cnn.com/2007/writers/the_bonus/09/11/ nascar/index.html.
Golenbock, Peter. *The Last Lap Updated: The Life and Times of NASCAR's Legendary Heroes*. New York: Hungry Minds, Inc., 2001.
---. *NASCAR Confidential*. St Paul, MN: Motorbooks International, 2004.
"H.A. Wheeler." *Wikipedia, the free encyclopedia*. http://en.wikipedia.org/wiki/Humpy_ Wheeler.
Higgins, Tom. "An Australian Adventure, Part V." *Tom Higgins' Scuffs*. ThatsRacin. com. 18 March 2008. http://blogs.thatsracin.com/scuffs/2008/03/an- australian-1.html.
---. "Bill Elliott Was Well up to the Long Journey." *Tom Higgins' Scuffs*.

ThatsRacin.com. 29 Nov. 2007. http://blogs.thatsracin.com/scuffs/2007/11/index. html.

---. "Daytona by the Decades." *Tom Higgins' Scuffs*. ThatsRacin.com. 9 Jan. 2008. http://blogs. thatsracin.com/scuffs/2008/01/index.html.

---. "Even with 10 Grand in Bodywork, the Gray Ghost Was Worth It." *Tom Higgins' Scuffs*. ThatsRacin.com. 7 Feb. 2006. http://blogs.thatsracin.com.scuffs/2006/02/even_ with_10_gr.html.

---. "A King Is Born." *Tom Higgins' Scuffs*. ThatsRacin.com. 24 Sept. 2007. http://blogs. thatsracin.com/scuffs/2007/09/index.html.

---. "Metcalfe, Mark Maker." *Tom Higgins' Scuffs*. ThatsRacin.com. 4 Sept. 2007. http://blogs. thatsracin.com/scuffs/2007/09/index.html.

---. "No Green and No Peanuts No Longer the Rule." *Tom Higgins' Scuffs*. ThatsRacin.com. 19 Sept. 2007. http://blogs.thatsracin.com/scuffs/2007/09/index.html.

---. "A Scene Seared in Memory." *Tom Higgins' Scuffs*. ThatsRacin.com. 12 Sept. 2007. http:// blogs.thatsracin.com/scuffs/2007/09/index.html.

---. "We're Having a Heat Wave." *Tom Higgins' Scuffs*. ThatsRacin.com. 7 Aug. 2007. http:// blogs.thatsracin.com/scuffs/2007/08/index.html.

Jensen, Tom. "Jeff Gordon: Chasing Shadows." *SPEEDtv.com*. 17 Nov. 2007. http://nascar. speedtv.com/article/jeff_gordon_chasing_shadows.

"Johnson Breaks Through for First Win." *Sports Illustrated*. 13 April 2008. http://sports illustrated.cnn.com/2008/racing/04/13/nascar.phoenix.ap/index.html.

Johnson, Kris. "Newmans Saving Lives of Dogs Across America." *The Ryan Newman Foundation*. 19 Feb. 2008. http://www.ryannewsmanfoundation.org/news/2008/ 02222008.htm.

Lage, Larry. "NASCAR's Mayfield Regrets Decisions When He Was 'Young and Dumb.'" *DailyJournalOnline Sports*. 23 Aug. 2007. http://www.mydjconnection.com/ articles/2007/08/23/sports/doc46cda9a757890288965712.txt.

Mallozzi, Vincent M. "NASCAR Flag Is Planted at the Top of the World." *The New York Times*. 9 Sept. 2007. http://www.nytimes.com/2007/09/09/sports/othersports/09cheer. html.

---. "Years of Thunder for Woman Called Lightning." *The New York Times*. 25 Nov. 2007. http://www.nytimes.com/2007/11/25/sports/othersports/25cheer.html.

Margolis, Bob. "No Regrets." *Yahoo!Sports*. 14 March 2008. http://sports.yahoo.com/nascar/ news.

Martin, Bruce. "NASCAR's Official Accident Report -- No. 3 Car." *hotrod.com*. http://www. hotrod.com/thehistoryof/nascar_accident_report_dale_earnhardt/index.html.

McCormick, Steve. "Bill France Jr." *About.com: NASCAR Racing*. http://nascar.about.com/ od/nascarhistory/p/billfrancejr.htm.

Menzer, Joe. *The Wildest Ride: A History of NASCAR*. New York: Touchstone, 2001.

Moses, Sam. "Dick Trickle Is NASCAR's Newest Good Ol' Boy." *Sports Illustrated*. 11 Dec. 1989. http://vault.sportsillustrated.cnn.com/vault/article/magazine/MAG1069208/ index.htm.

---. "If You Can't Prove It, You Ain't It." *Sports Illustrated*. 17 Oct. 1977. http://vault.sports illustrated.cnn.com/vault/article/magazine/MAG1092910/index.htm.

---. "Nice Meetin' Ya, The Name's Cale." *Sports Illustrated*. 6 Nov. 1978. http://vault.sport sillustrated.cnn.com/vault/article/magazine/MAG1094277/index.htm.

"NASCAR Mourns the Intimidator: Memorial Service Held in Dale Earnhardt's Memory." *CBSNews.com*. 22 Feb. 2001. http://www.cbsnews.com/stories/2001/02/21/sports/ main273652.

"Ned Jarrett." *howstuffworks.com*. http://entertainment.howstuffworks.com/ned-jarrett.htm.

"Ned Jarrett." *Wikipedia, the free encyclopedia*. http://en.wikipedia.org/wiki/Ned_Jarrett.

Newton, David. "Junior Johnson Remains Active as a Father, Farmer." *NASCAR.com*. 31 July 2006. http://www.nascar.com/2006/news/features/lifestyle/07/31/junior.johnson/

index.html.

---. "NASCAR No Place for Women . . . Until Guthrie." *NASCAR.com.* 26 May 2006. http://www.nascar.com.2006/news/headlines/cup/05/26/jguthrie.women.nascar/index.html.

Pantellere, Sean. "Pit Crew Renaissance." *Auto Racing Scene.* 2 March 2007. http://www.autoracingscene.com/articles_030207_pit_crew_renaissance.

Poole, David. "Helton Turned Life into Lessons." *Life in the Turn Lane.* 31 March 2008. http://turn-lane.blogspot.com.

Poole, David and Jim McLaurin. *"Then Junior Said to Jeff . . .": The Best NASCAR Stories Ever Told.* Chicago: Triumph Books, 2006.

"Quotebook: Chase for the Nextel Cup Drivers." *NASCAR.com.* 31 Oct. 2004. http://www.nascar.com/2004/news/headlines/cup/10/31/atlanta_quotes/index.html.

"Reutimann Says Goodbye to a Good Home in the NASCAR Craftsman Truck Series." *toyota.com.* 13 Nov. 2006. http://www.toyota.com/motorsports/ncts/news/2006/11-13-06-01.html.

"Richard Petty." Wikipedia, the free encyclopedia. http://en.wikipedia.org/wiki/Richard_Petty.

Ross, Alan. "King Richard Rules." *AmericanProfile.com.* 30 Jan. 2005. http://www.americanprofile.com/article/4561.html.

Rovell, Darren. "Carl Edwards Could Be Next Big Star of NASCAR." *CNBC.com.* 10 March 2008. http://www.cnbc.com/id/23557255.

Samples, Steve. "Herman the Turtle." *Beyond the Grandstand.* 2 Jan. 2002. http://www.gordonline.com/beyond/010202.html.

"Sensational NASCAR Crash." angrybrownguy.com. 5 April 2008. http://www.angrybrownguy.com/?p=257.

Severson, Kim. "At 190 M.P.H., Who Needs a Spare Tire?" *The New York Times.* 14 June 2006. http://www.nytimes.com/2006/06/14/dining/14nasc.html.

Smith, Marty. "Junior: 'Sometimes the Hero Is Built Up to Be Torn Down.'" *NASCAR.com.* http://www.nascar.com/special/earnhardt/stories/interview.html.

Smith, Steven Cole. "NASCAR Fans: Be Careful When You Talk 'Tradition.'" *Edmunds Inside Line.* 16 Feb. 2007. http://www.edmunds.com/insideline/do/Columns/articleId=19633.

"Sterling Marlin," *Wikipedia, the free encyclopedia.* http://en.wikipedia.org/wiki/Sterling_Marlin.

Sturbin, John. "The NASCAR Super Team: Hendrick Motorsports." *Star-Telegraph.com.* 13 April 2008. http://www.star-telegram.com/sports/story/561705.html.

Swan, Raygan. "Who Are You Wearing? Pits the 'It' Place for Fashion." *NASCAR.com.* 22 Feb. 2008. http://www.hobbytalk.com/bbs1/showthread.php?t=211886.

Swift, Earl. "The Story Behind the Scar of Norfolk's Early NASCAR Hero." *The Virginian-Pilot.* 2 Oct. 2007. http://www.joeweatherly.com/Stories.htm.

"Texas: Toyota NASCAR Nationwide Race Recap, Quotes." *PaddockTalk.* 5 April 2008. http://www.paddocktalk.com/news/html.

Zweig, Eric. ***. Buffalo, NY: Firefly Books, 2007. (The title is not suitable for publication here; for the book's title, contact the author.)

INDEX
(LAST NAME, DEVOTION DAY NUMBER)